Global Perspectives Series

Grieving with Hope

Langham

GLOBAL LIBRARY

Here is a study of preaching at funerals which is timely and important. At a time when many have lost confidence in the proclamation of Christian hope at the time of death, this book offers a corrective to such hesitancy. It does so by careful theological and pastoral consideration of the task, and it offers practical guidance and suggestions to those who stand before a congregation to declare God's word in the face of death. Dr Masarik has done us an invaluable service.

Rev Paul Sheppy, PhD
Former Research Fellow, Regent's Park College, University of Oxford, UK
Former Secretary, Joint Liturgical Group of Great Britain

This is a unique work of its kind. In both the Catholic and Protestant theological setting there are currently very few works like it. The author is responding to both the hearers' receptiveness as well as the possibilities afforded by the church in its mission. It is apparent that it is inappropriate in a funeral setting to overwhelm the hearers with too much teaching on eschatological themes. It is important to recognize the hearers' tendency to pose questions and to answer these in the light of the gospel. Thanks to the author having studied many foreign works, Dr Masarik has enriched Slovak theological literature with many insights.

Professor Anton Fabian, PhD
Professor, Catholic Theology, Ružomberok, Slovakia

In all sections of this work, Dr Masarik utilizes a broad selection of literature of both national and foreign (English and German) origin, which he uses to reinforce the assertions and opinions presented.

Above all, though, we should call attention to the author's skill in combining all his study efforts in a synthetized work, including scholarship-funded trips and participation in academic projects. The clarity of the work and its line of reasoning are the best evidence of this.

The work may be also considered to be stimulating for expert discussion, offering direction for a presentation of views concerning the issue of funeral sermons. Thanks are due the author for his "view from the end," which also opens up discussion on the level of all of society, for example, that it is our common task to look for the best model of life for all people and not Christians alone.

This book will certainly serve the wide community of clergy of all churches, students of theology, lay speakers at funeral ceremonies, and others. I found this book very enriching and was personally deeply touched by it. My sincere thanks to Dr Masarik for this work.

Professor Jozef Jarab, PhD
Head of the Catholic University in Ružomberok, Slovakia

Grieving with Hope is Dr Albín Masarik's second work on the topic of funeral sermons. Like the first, it is rare in the publishing arena of Slovak theology and in my opinion, its research is highly relevant and needed for the area of theology.

I would like to call attention to the author's originality, especially in sections treating the pastoral framework for homiletic activity, the possibilities for nonverbal communication of gospel attitudes, the increase of the message's relevance and its potential impact, as well as reinforcement of the preacher's authenticity. He presents the solutions on offer with an eye to lessening the stress not only of the bereaved, but also of the preachers themselves. The work is conceived in an ecumenical spirit with sensitivity for differing Christian traditions and their usual terminology. Dr Masarik has shown competence in systematic academic research. He wrote the work submitted here on the basis of results attained by processing reliable and empirically verified information, after thorough preparation and an appropriate selection of scientific findings. His method of interpreting the facts and of preparing the ensuing results for publication prompts me to consider the important work presented of great value and benefit.

Professor Pavel Procházka, PhD
Department of Theology and Christian Education,
Faculty of Education, Matej Bel University, Banska Bystrica, Slovakia

This book is an excellent contribution to the question of funeral sermons. It is very rich, written at a high level, but also comprehensible. Dr Masarik has succeeded in integrating several important facets, like counselling, as well. Focused on the main issues, it will surely be very helpful for ministry!

Professor Birgit Weyel, PhD
Chair of Practical Theology,
Evangelisch-Theologische Fakultät, Eberhard Karls Universität, Tübingen, Germany

Grieving with Hope by Dr Albín Masarik is a welcome addition to our churches and will provide much enrichment for pastors. Generations of pastors will return to it as they prepare their funeral sermons. Particularly admirable is the analytical detail used in bringing out masterful aspects of the problems encountered in bereavement and the theological aspects of the problem.

I am convinced that this work will enrich libraries in many churches. Our Slovak theology has once again spoken!

Professor Igor Kišš, ThDr
Former Dean, Evangelical Faculty of Theology,
Comenius University, Bratislava, Slovakia

Grieving with Hope

Selected Aspects of Funeral Sermons

Albín Masarik

Langham

GLOBAL LIBRARY

© 2017 Albín Masarik

Published 2017 by Langham Global Library
An imprint of Langham Publishing
www.langhampublishing.org

Langham Publishing and its imprints are a ministry of Langham Partnership

Langham Partnership
PO Box 296, Carlisle, Cumbria, CA3 9WZ, UK
www.langham.org

ISBNs:
978-1-78368-377-2 Print
978-1-78368-383-3 ePub
978-1-78368-384-0 Mobi
978-1-78368-385-7 PDF

British Library Cataloguing in Publication Data
A catalogue record for this book is available from the British Library

ISBN: 978-1-78368-377-2

Cover & Book Design: projectluz.com

Translation: Graham Peter Leeder
Translation of this book was carried out with the financial help of the PROMET SLOVAKIA, s.r.o., Radlinského 1730, 02601 Dolný Kubín, Slovakia.

Reviewers:
Mons. Prof. ThDr. JCDr. Anton Fabian, PhD.
Prof. ThDr. Jozef Jarab, PhD.
Prof. ThDr. Pavel Procházka, PhD

CONTENTS

Preface..ix

Acknowledgements...xi

Introduction...1
    Defining the Topic   1
    Explanation of the Topic Choice   2
    Referenced Literature   3
    Aims   8
    Methods   9

1   Definitions, Theological Justification, and Typological Specifics of
Funeral Sermons...11
    The Definition of a Funeral Sermon   11
    Theological Justification of Funeral Sermons   14
    Typological Specifications of Funeral Sermons   15

2   The Homiletical Situation of a Funeral.................................25
    The Terms "Differentiation" and "the Homiletical Situation"   25
    Questions and Stimuli for Determining the Homiletical Situation   27
    Facets of the Homiletical Situation   29

3   The Purpose of Funeral Sermons......................................61
    Purpose of Funeral Sermons as a Part of a Church Service   61
    The Purpose of Funeral Sermons as a Part of the Funeral   63
    The Funeral Sermon as a Proclamation of the Word in a Specific
    Homiletical Situation   69

4   The Homiletical Process..101
    The Stages of Preparing a Funeral Sermon   101
    Forms of Expression   128
    Structure and Length of the Funeral Sermon   131
    Non-Kerygmatic and Kerygmatic Components of Funeral Sermons   136
    Details about the Deceased Person   138

Conclusion...153

Bibliography...157

Index..165

Preface

Funeral preaching maintains a special place among the tasks of a minister for at least two reasons:

1. *It is one of the broadest forms of contact that the church has with the general public.* Friends, neighbours, and colleagues of the deceased or the bereaved will attend a church funeral regardless of their differing religious attitudes. Therefore, a church funeral can be an opportunity for the church to communicate with the non-church public as well as with believers from different Christian traditions.

2. *It remains a marginal theoretical interest of theologians.* This is true both in relation to the production of theoretical publications as well as to the creation of university textbooks for the subject of situational homiletics in the Slovak Republic. Published collections of funeral sermons are a valuable aide to the minister, but they do not address theoretical questions. An uncritical use of these collections may even create a further independent set of problems.

The interrelationship between these two contradictory facts is noteworthy and seems difficult to explain. Ministers find themselves in a significant and demanding part of their ministry without direct theological support. Such support ought to be based on a true picture of how the gospel is currently preached at funerals and its analysis from a theological and wider interdisciplinary perspective. In this book, I am attempting to contribute to the development of the theoretical basis for situational homiletics in two areas:

1. In the theoretical field – to open a wider theological (and preferably also interdisciplinary) discussion which will help to identify the current strengths and weaknesses in this area of our ministry.

2. In the practical field – an attempt to find a way that would realistically raise ministers' expectations about the significance of their ministry and that they would attempt to undertake the tasks of situational homiletics with a broader perspective.[1]

---

1. This is why the conclusions of the Homiletical Course in Vienna (1911) are valuable. P. Zemko states: "Dr. Köck emphasised that the principles of the Vienna Homiletical Course form the basis for the requirements for further education of the preachers of God's Word and

This work cannot claim to be a comprehensive treatment of the whole topic, but it does theology to the benefit of the Christian ministry of proclaiming the gospel. If it in some way contributes to more contemporary funeral sermons achieving their aims, then my efforts were not in vain.

homiletical texts should be a valid aid for the preparation of spiritual addresses, but they must not be used slavishly as the minister should strive to work independently." *Homiletické směrnice. Z dějin homiletiky na Moravě, v Čechách a na Slovensku* (Trnava: Dobrá kniha, 2007), 23.

Acknowledgements

First of all, I wish to express my sincere gratitude to God that I can work on this topic which I believe is deeply meaningful. I started out my research with the theological expectations of obtaining new homiletical findings and with the Christian faith that both preaching the Word of God and the community of faith have a real impact when dealing with a serious loss, as is the case in the death of a loved one. This approach stems from the nature of the gospel and from the creative impact of God's Word in the life of a Christian.

This work builds on my own previous homiletical research conducted on the funeral sermons of Prof ThDr Igor Kišš. I owe him a great debt of gratitude that he was prepared to take a risk and allow me to analyze certain features of his funeral sermons. Through a critical approach to his collection, I obtained my first set of real attributes of contemporary (evangelical) funeral sermons in Slovakia and identified significant points and questions that could aid the development and improvement of current practice.

I am also grateful to all those who read and reacted to my "analysis," be they the reviewers of academic publications (Mgr Jozef Benka, PhD; Prof ThDr Imre Peres, PhD; and Prof ThDr Pavel Procházka, PhD) or the commendations on the book cover (Prof ThDr Jozef Jarab, PhD and Prof ThDr ICDr Anton Fabián, PhD). Without their insights, I would have probably overlooked a number of problems.

I would also like to thank my colleagues at the Department of Theology and Christian Education, Pedagogical Faculty, Matej Bel University in Banská Bystrica, as they create a stimulating environment which has facilitated many conversations that were for me like valuable consultations. I would like to thank by name my colleague, who is currently the moderator of the ministry board of the Brethren Church of Slovakia, ThDr Ing Ján Henžel, PhD, who for the purpose of my research provided me with a collection of over forty of his funeral sermons.

I also wish to show my appreciation to the aforementioned Professor Pavel Procházka, not only for his help in processing the preliminary study to this work but also that from his position as the head of department, during the summer semester 2007/08, he offered me the opportunity of a four-month study scholarship at Belfast Bible College (part of Queen's University) in Belfast. The time in Northern Ireland was implemented and funded using scholarship funds of that college, for which I also wish to express my gratitude. During my participation in the training program for theology teachers, I had the conditions that enabled me to write this work. Viewed from the perspective of the topic, my conversations with their teacher of homiletics, Ian Dickson PhD, were of great benefit. His research focuses on Irish church sermons from the nineteenth century, and he has made a number of observations about how the proclamation of the Word influences society. As I was studying his subject, he also helped me by allowing me to lecture about parts of my research and respond to the thoughts of his students.

In the process of writing this work, I also wrote to a number of institutes and individuals. An example is Paul Sheppy from Reading, UK. As for the purposes of this study I had taken into account his publications which deal with the question of the liturgical and pastoral context of a funeral. I would like to thank him for the valuable advice he provided in his letter.

With regard to those who work with the bereaved and organize funerals, I would like to thank Jim Clark. He grew up in a family who owned a funeral home in Bangor, Northern Ireland, and so that he would be able to develop their funeral services, he studied theology at university. He allowed me to visit him which enabled me to view this rather unique combination of business activity and pastoral ministry. During my visit, he met with a client whom he served not only as the owner of a funeral home but also as a qualified Christian pastoral worker. Therefore, from this visit to his funeral home, I left with the hope that there is significance in paying attention to the question of improving the quality of Christian ministry to the grieving.

I would also like to express my gratitude to the head of the crematorium in Banská Bystrica, Pavol Bielik, who agreed to my request to carry out field observations, which consisted of attending one hundred funerals, making a sound recording, and communicating with the person who conducted the funeral. I also cannot fail to mention Mgr Halaj, a civil funeral celebrant, who valiantly endured my presence at his funerals and was willing to discuss all the points I raised in connection with his work.

Thanks also belong to the civic organization Človek človeku (Person to Person), which directs the methodological aspect of civil funerals in Slovakia. I formed a friendly relationship with their general secretary, Ján Milkáš, and we exchanged the results of our work. This enabled me to study authentic methodological material which this organization publishes to support groups organizing civil affairs in Slovak towns and villages. While doing this, certain questions sprung to mind which a funeral must come to terms with, regardless of whether its starting point is religious or non-religious.

I would like to express my gratitude to all the bereaved who were open to speaking about their loss and about their perceptions of the funeral. We talked about what was significant for them and about what bothered or stressed them. As a part of this group, I would also like to mention the students from the Social and Missionary Workers with the Roma Community course during the winter semester of 2007/08 at the external campus of the Education Faculty of the University of Matej Bel in Rimavská Sobota. After I had lectured about the issue of pastoral care for the dying and bereaved, a number of them evaluated in their seminar work, experiences from their families of dying, and coming to terms with the loss. This allowed me to view a wide range of experiences of loss and the various ways which the bereaved created to process it. Some of these approaches revealed the significance their Christian faith in God has for them, while other approaches were theologically questionable. But the bereaved do not always experience their loss in ways the minister expects them to. They process it on the basis of their cultural, religious, and social assumptions. The occurrence of problematic Christian approaches in a Christian context can be connected to a lack of church support for the bereaved. Due to the constraints of this work, I will not be able to analyze them here, but situational homiletics as a discipline cannot afford to overlook them.

Finally, I would like to express my thankfulness to Graham Peter Leeder, my translator, and to Promet Slovakia, Ltd., for their financial support of this translation. Very special thanks belongs also to Pieter Kwant, director of Langham Literature, for his help and encouragement, and to Vivian Doub, who gave me many suggestions and support. Cooperation with her was a very unique experience on the way to the English version of this book. Many thanks.

Introduction

Defining the Topic

The subtitle of this book, *Selected Aspects of Funeral Sermons,* states the subject and field of research. It expresses that this work belongs to the field of homiletics which is part of practical theology. The field can be even more narrowly defined as part of situational homiletics,[1] and from this it is limited to one topical area – funeral sermons. This means that this work does not cover all the issues of homiletics, not even the whole field of situational homiletics, but it is focused on one specific field – funeral sermons. It is based on my own observations and their analysis taking into account academic discourse. As I am analyzing my subject in the form of a study that is based on observations (theory – from the Greek verb *theōrein* – observe), it defines the problems and their opportunities and risks and offers a broader analysis of the theoretical questions connected to funeral sermons from different perspectives along with their specific problems. At the same time, it means that this work does not take the form of a guide that enables instant preparation of a funeral sermon.

---

1. According to P. Zemko, in Roman Catholic homiletics this field is referred to as "special homiletics" (*Homiletické směrnice. Z dějin homiletiky na Moravě, v Čechách a na Slovensku* [Trnava: Dobrá kniha, 2007], 66). In support of the use of the term "situational" (from the Latin *casus* – case) as a technical term, it is possible to refer to Prof J. Smolík, who uses this term to refer to proclamation at church services which are due to life events of individual members of the church. See J. Smolík, *Radost ze slova,* 148: "In addition to church services around the word and the sacraments there are church services for different 'situations.' Situations (weddings, funerals) that could be included in Sunday church services. That this does not happen is more down to technical rather than principled considerations." This term is also used in the Orthodox church by for example P. O. Axman and P. Aleš (*Homiletika.* [Olomouc: Pravoslavná Bohoslovecká Fakulta Prešovské Univerzity v Prešově, Detašované pracoviště v Olomouci, 2003], 82): "There are a number of church events during which the address has a dominant position, because it is necessary to preach God's Word. Preaching at these proceedings is entitled occasional or situational (Latin *casus* = case)."

Explanation of the Topic Choice

Funeral preaching is one of the most difficult parts of a minister's work. This statement is supported by a large collection of authors,[2] and I have yet to find one source which would cast doubt on this stance. On the contrary, ministers from a range of churches in Slovakia have in conversation indicated that they regard ministering at funerals as a burden, and some of those would rather avoid it. I have also come across the case of a theology graduate who tried to find out if it is possible to be ordained to the ministry with the exception that he "wouldn't have to conduct funerals."

On the other hand, there are ministers who state that they do not have a problem with funerals and that they are able to handle them competently. While reflecting on this group of ministers, I asked the question, does "competently handling" mean that they take into consideration all the theological implications and relevantly present them in that specific homiletic situation, or does it just mean that the minister does not feel any need to come to terms with any problems in regard to funeral sermons? Only very rarely do I encounter a minister who regards this part of his work as a privilege and a significant part of his ministry. An example of such an exception is C. Stebler who states, "It is increasingly becoming clear to me how privileged I am. It is a privilege to be able to accompany people of all ages in grieving, through periods of life that are extremely intense and where a lot is at stake."[3]

If my observations are objective, then these experiences could indicate that ministers are as yet not fully aware of the ministry possibilities that open up for them at funerals and in funeral sermons. It could also indicate other problems of a more personal nature (e.g. not having come to terms with the reality of their own mortality or an inability to empathetically process impressions from the funeral context), or of a theological-professional nature (e.g. an inadequate anchoring in biblical eschatology, soteriology, etc.). Therefore, it is necessary

---

2. See for example *Agenda ČCE* (Agenda of the Evangelical Church of Czech Brethren [ECCB], 1983), 194: "Funeral sermons are one of the most difficult types of sermons." Similarly J. Jamnický states: "One of the hardest problems in practical theology is the question of funeral sermons. Alongside the problem of church discipline there isn't in practical theology a problem which is more difficult to solve than this one." *Evanjelické pohrebné kázne* (Liptovský sv. Mikuláš: Tranoscius, 1927), 1. Similar is stated by K. Willhite: "During my years of pastoral ministry, I found few circumstances more challenging or rewarding than memorial services." "Introduction, Part Two, Funerals," in *A Contemporary Handbook for Weddings and Funerals and Other Occasions*, ed. A. Malphurs and K. Willhite (Grand Rapids: Kregel, 2003), 149.

3. Ch. Stebler, *Die drei Dimensionen der Bestattungspredigt, Theologie, Biographie und Trauergemeinde* (Zürich: Theologisker Verlag, 2006), 13.

to pay considerably more attention to this topic as a part of internal church life and during theological education, before beginning ministry but also as a part of a lifelong programme of learning. At the same time, I believe that it is not enough to just pay more attention to this problem. It also requires the courage to take a deep, critical look – both from the perspective of practical theology as well as part of broader interdisciplinary discussions. Without a critical evaluation of current practice and consideration of the foundational objectives of funeral preaching, we only achieve a reduction in the subjective feeling of stress caused by conducting these services, or alternatively a greater variability in the style of our wording, which is what Kišš attempts.[4] These would serve a purpose, but they wouldn't necessarily lead to an objective improvement in quality. This is why I want to move our thinking towards an intentional handling of the funeral preaching task.

Referenced Literature

In the academic literature, we find a large number of titles which deal with this topic from both a religious[5] and non-religious standpoint.[6] From a religious position, the side of Christian theology, we find works of varying type and scope from (1) monographs, to (2) chapters in books, to (3) scientific, academic, and popular articles.

Foundational Homiletical Starting Points and Situational-Homiletical Monographs

Foundational homiletical starting points. Situational homiletics is unable to develop independently from foundational homiletical approaches. For this reason, during the preparation of this work I referred to a number of textbooks of homiletics. From Roman Catholic authors, special mention should be given

---

4. I. Kišš states, "in the churches of some priests there are many funerals and at every funeral there are many members of the general public in attendance. It is therefore necessary to have new topics for funeral sermons so that there is variety." *Nádej nad hrobom, 1.-4. časť* (Pohrebné kázne, Bratislava, 1995–96, vlastný náklad), 2.

5. When monitoring religious starting points, this study is limited to those of churches represented in Slovakia. Non-Christian religions and Christian communities that are not registered according to the law of registration of churches and religious organizations will not be studied.

6. A non-religious approach to the topic is represented for example by the publications of the Slovak association Person to Person (Človek človeku), whose aim is to support the development of high quality civil ceremonies in Slovakia.

to the extensive work of J. Vrablec and A. Fabián, *Homiletika I.–II. základná a materiálna* (*Homiletics I–II: Foundations and Material*).[7] From the Protestant context, I worked particularly with the homiletical works of Rudolf Bohren, *Predigtlehre* (Homiletics); Haddon W. Robinson, *Biblical Preaching*; and Adolf Pohl, *Anleitung zum Predigen* (Instructions about preaching).[8]

Homiletical works with a particular emphasis. From the work of M. Šuráb, the most significant for the topic of funeral sermons is his monograph, *Terapeutický rozmer homílie* (The therapeutic dimension of the homily).[9] Even though funeral sermons are not his direct focus, his study on the therapeutic impact of sermons is clearly relevant to the proclamation of the gospel at funerals. Therefore, in future research it will be necessary to pay greater attention to his work, and in order to establish a connection between his questions and results and the proclamation of the gospel at funerals. The same is true about the work of A. Fabián, *Utrpenie má aj iný rozmer* (Suffering also has another dimension).[10]

The study from P. Zemko, *Homiletické směrnice: Z dějin homiletiky na Moravě, v Čechách a na Slovensku* (Homiletical directives from the history of homiletics in Moravia, the Czech Republic, and Slovakia), is very inspiring. But its treatment of funeral sermons only refers to the systematic classification of the discipline, and funeral sermons are regarded as belonging to the field of special homiletics.[11]

Collections of funeral sermons. From Roman Catholic authors, there is a collection, *Pohrebné kázne* (Funeral Homilies), by Stanček, which provides a set of funeral sermons but does not address any questions relating to situational-homiletical theory.[12] A similar work is J. Jurko's aid to funeral addresses, *Verím,*

---

7. J. Vrablec and A. Fabián, *Homiletika I.–II. základná a materiálna* (Trnava: SSV, 2001).

8. R. Bohren, *Predigtlehre* (München: Kaiser, 1980); H. Robinson, *Biblical Preaching* (Grand Rapids: Baker, 1980); A. Pohl, *Anleitung zum Predigen: ein Arbeitsheft für Predigthelfer* (Wuppertal und Kasel: Oncken Verlag, 1979).

9. M. Šuráb, *Terapeutický rozmer homílie* (Bratislava: Vydavateľstvo spolku slovenských spisovateľov, spol. p.r.o. pre Rímskokatolícku cyrilometodskú bohosloveckú fakultu, UK, 2008).

10. A. Fabián, *Utrpenie má aj iný rozmer* (Prešov: Vydavateľstvo Michala Vaška, 1999).

11. P. Zemko, *Homiletické směrnice. Z dějin homiletiky na Moravě, v Čechách a na Slovensku* (Trnava: Dobrá kniha, 2007). On page 65, he presents a possible division of Roman Catholic homiletics, and on page 66, he states that in special homiletics, there are four types of spiritual addresses. In the second group, sermons according to their purpose, he includes "funeral, wedding and baptismal."

12. Ľ. Stanček, *Pohrebné homílie* (Spišská Kapitula – Spišské Podhradie: Kňazský seminár biskupa Jána Vojtaššáka, 2003).

že môj Vykupiteľ žije (I believe that my redeemer lives).[13] Both of these works could make a contribution to the theory of situational homiletics if they were critically analyzed.

From the Lutheran church, reference can be made to Igor Kišš's collection of funeral sermons *Nádej nad hrobom I.–IV* (Hope that overcomes the grave).[14] Just before this work was completed, I obtained another Lutheran collection of funeral sermons: *Potešujte sa vospolok týmito slovami. Zbierka pohrebných príhovorov evanjelických a.v.duchovných* (Comfort the brethren with these words: A collection of funeral addresses by Lutheran ministers).[15] This collection does not contain observations in relation to situational homiletics, but it is a collection of several ministers' work which provides a picture of the current state of funeral sermons in the Lutheran church and could serve as an excellent dataset for future research.

Monographs about funeral sermons

Slovak monographs. In 1927, Prof Ján Jamincký published the monograph, *Evanjelické pohrebné kázne: Homiletická úvaha* (Lutheran funeral sermons: A Homiletical reflection).[16] It was his doctoral thesis and is divided into four parts: (1) Funeral liturgy; (2) Funeral preaching as a sacred act; (3) The contents of funeral sermons; and (4) Texts and formats of funeral sermons. This work is highly critical of the state of funeral sermons in his day and searches for possibly ways to rectify the situation.

In the range of monographs dealing with this topic, there is also my own work, *Analýza nekérygmatických komponentov pohrebných kázní prof. Igora Kišša* (An analysis of the non-kerygmatic component of the funeral sermons of Prof Igor Kišš).[17] It is an analysis of the textual content of a set of fifty-four funeral sermons from Prof Igor Kišš and, as well as an introduction and conclusion, it consists of the following chapters: (1) The homiletical situation and elements of homiletical differentiation; (2) The choice of sermon text and homiletical differentiation; (3) A general introduction to funeral sermons; (4) Addressing the bereaved; and (5) The sermon conclusion – parting

---

13. J. Jurko, *Verím, že môj Vykupiteľ žije. Pomôcka k pohrebným príhovorom* (Kapušany: Ing. Štefánia Beňová - Bens, 2000).

14. I. Kišš, *Nádej nad hrobom, 1.–4. časť.*

15. M. Šefranko and R. Cingeľ, *Potešujte sa vospolok týmito slovami. Zbierka pohrebných príhovorov evanjelických a.v.duchovných* (Bratislava/Prešov: ZED, 2009).

16. J. Jamnický, *Evanjelické pohrebné kázne.*

17. A. Masarik, *Analýza nekérygmatických komponentov pohrebných kázní prof. Igora Kišša* (Banská Bystrica: PF UMB, 2008).

with the hope of the resurrection. My aim in this study was to identify the potential components of a funeral sermon, and I paid attention to all parts of the structure and wording of the funeral sermons, apart from the so-called "sermon in the stricter sense of the word" (i.e. the delivery of the message of the text). The results obtained from the analysis of Kišš's sermons are being used in the writing of this work.

International monographs. From international monographs, special mention should be given to the following publications. Based on what I have discovered, the work completed for the highest academic degree on this topic is the habilitation thesis of Berger, *Die christliche Botschaft von Tod und Auferstehung und ihre Verkündigung am Grabe*, from Berlin in 1963.[18] Unfortunately, I have been unable to gain access to this work, so I have been unable to build on his results. I have had more success obtaining the works of P. Sheppy, *Death Liturgy and Ritual, vol. 1, A Pastoral and Liturgical Theology; Death Liturgy and Ritual, vol. 2, A Commentary on Liturgical Texts*; and *In Sure and Certain Hope.*[19] His works were for me of great importance. I can say something similar about the works of Wesley Carr, *Brief Encounters: Pastoral Ministry through Baptism, Weddings and Funerals* and *Handbook of Pastoral Studies: Learning and Practising Christian Ministry*, which I thoroughly studied and gained a lot of valuable material from.[20] I also wish to mention the published dissertation of C. Stebler, *Die drei Dimensionen der Bestattungspredigt* (The three dimensions of the funeral sermon), which clearly demonstrates the necessity of reflecting on three areas: theology, the specifics of each case, and those attending the funeral.[21]

Chapters of Books That Address Funeral Sermons

From Slovak authors who address the topic of funeral sermons within their books, mention should be made again of Kišš's theoretical section in his

---

18. H. Berger, *Die christliche Botschaft von Tod und Auferstehung und ihre Verkündigung am Grabe* (Habilitation thesis, Berlin 10.6.1963).

19. P. Sheppy, *Death Liturgy and Ritual, vol. 1, A Pastoral and Liturgical Theology* (Aldershot, UK: Ashgate, 2003); *Death Liturgy and Ritual, vol. 2, A Commentary on Liturgical Texts* (Aldershot, UK: Ashgate, 2004); *In Sure and Certain Hope: Liturgies, Prayers and Readings for Funerals and Memorials* (Norwich, UK: Canterbury Press, 2003).

20. W. Carr, *Brief Encounters: Pastoral Ministry through Baptism, Weddings and Funerals*, rev. ed. (London: SPCK, 1994); *Handbook of Pastoral Studies: Learning and Practising Christian Ministry* (London: SPCK, 1997).

21. Ch. Stebler, *Die drei Dimensionen.*

collection of sermons *Nádej nad hrobom I–IV* (Hope that overcomes the grave).[22] This theoretical study of 1,200 words is dedicated to the questions of both the formal structure and the emphasis of funeral sermons. In a practical way, it characterizes the separate tasks and points out the potential risks. From the Lutherans, I would mention Prof J. Filo's reflection on funeral sermons, *Evanjeliové možnosti a problematika pohrebnej kázne* (Gospel possibilities and the problems of funeral sermons) in the published collection of his father, J. Filo Sr, *Pohľady do neba* (Glimpses of heaven).[23] This work deals with the question of the foundational theological objectives of a funeral and the sermon, where the objectives are defined as: (1) help in a difficult life situation; (2) encouraging faith; and (3) missionary address. This is followed by a focus on the specifically Christian content of the graveside address, the relationship of the sermon to the deceased person, and the choice of biblical text.

From the Orthodox church, P. O. Axman and P. Aleš deal with the topic of funeral sermons in *Homiletika* (Homiletics).[24] Even though it is a Czech work, I have included it the Slovak section as it originated at an external campus of the University of Prešov.

From the foreign literature that deals with the topic at the level of a chapter, I mostly make use of the following: *Handbuch der Praktischen Theologie II* (Handbook of Practical Theology, vol. 2) which contains the study of H. H. Jenssen, *Die Kirchlichen Handlungen* (The ceremonies of the church).[25] It is a stimulating study which asks theoretical questions and addresses them in a way that is practical and applicable. Haddon Robinson and C. B. Larson were the general editors of *The Art and Craft of Biblical Preaching*, and in this work S. Rummage has a chapter entitled "Redemptive Sermons for Weddings and Funerals."[26] In this discussion, the material is divided up as follows: (1) Biblical content; (2) Personal appeal; (3) Abbreviated length; and (4) Redemptive purpose. This 715-page work dedicates only three pages to funeral and wedding sermons which I regard as a missed opportunity.

---

22. I. Kišš, *Nádej nad hrobom*, 1.–4.

23. J. Filo, *Pohľady do neba. Kázne, príhovory a rozlúčky pri pohreboch a pietnych príležitostiach* (Vydavateľstvo Michala Vaška, Prešov, 2004).

24. P. O. Axman and P. Aleš, *Homiletika*, 82–86.

25. H. H. Jenssen, *Die kirchliche Handlungen*, in *Handbuch der Praktischen Theologie, vol. 2* (Berlin: Evangelische Verlagsanstalt, 1979).

26. S. Rummage, "Redemptive Sermons for Weddings and Funerals: When the Sermon Is the Last Thing on Your Hearers' Minds," in *The Art and Craft of Biblical Preaching: A Comprehensive Resource for Today's Communicators*, ed. H. Robinson and C. B. Larson (Grand Rapids: Zondervan, 2005).

Academic Journal Articles about Funeral Sermons

I searched for academic journal articles concerning the question of funeral sermons, mainly through the database ATLA, using the search terms "funeral preaching," "funeral sermons," "occasional offices," "eulogy," and the like. Unfortunately, I was only able to access works which were available in the database in the full text form. The ones which I interacted with in this work are listed in the bibliography with full bibliographical details.

Aims

When working on the proposal for this work, I set ambitious aims – to contribute to the development of the theory of situational homiletics by attempting to answer selected theoretical questions about funeral sermons and to do so on the basis of my own situational homiletics research and theoretical reflection on the tabled problems. I attempted to use methods that meant that my work would contribute to both academic reflection and support a sustainable long-term improvement to actual preaching.

In pursuit of these aims in 2006/07, I first undertook a preliminary study. I analyzed a set of sermons from one minister in order to obtain an idea of the potential structures of funeral sermons. This study then served as a reference point for expanding the research sample to include more ministers from a range of churches. After that should have followed an expansion of the research on a survey of one hundred funeral addresses and sermons, which I planned to undertake through observations in the field that would be recorded and then theologically analyzed for the purposes of my work. After that I had planned to summarize the results of my research into a theoretical treatise in which I would not refer to my observations and sample but would have listed possible approaches with their opportunities and risks. However, the challenges of real life changed my plans. In the winter of 2007, I received an offer to take part in an international study visit to Belfast, Northern Ireland. Therefore, I changed the order of my steps.

I travelled to Northern Ireland with the expectation that I would have access to extensive resources, similar to what was available to me at Wheaton College in the USA, where I prepared the material for my doctoral thesis. The library of the school I was visiting was not in any sense focused on situational homiletics, and I was able to make only a limited use of interlibrary loans. A benefit, though, was access to the database ATLA, which I took full advantage of in order to aid the later critical discourse.

I undertook empirical research using a participational-observational method at one hundred funerals at the crematorium in Banská Bystrica, Slovakia, both before and during the preparation of this study. It served mainly as a way of collecting specific examples of funeral sermons to be used later when resolving theoretical questions. I regarded the approaches used by the ministers as my results, because they emanated either from a purposeful theoretical approach or in some cases from an intuitive observational approach. Both of course have the potential to contribute to the theoretical development of this discipline. Therefore, during the writing of the individual parts of this book, I have relied not only on the discussion found in the academic literature, but I have also tried to base it on approaches which I observed in practice.

Methods

To achieve the aims, the methods of analysis and synthesis are used in this work.

Analysis

When studying the partial and overall conclusions found in the literature relating to the subject of this work, an analytical approach was used, as well as when studying the stimuli from my own situational-homiletical research which was undertaken in two phases.

The first phase of the research, carried out using a method of content analysis of published collections of funeral sermons,[27] concentrated on mapping the structure of funeral sermons and the variable approaches to completing each separate task. The research potential of this first phase of work was that it equipped me with tools for the critical evaluation of the existing state of funeral sermons and provided a set of questions and working hypotheses for making further progress.

The second phase of the research, carried out using a field participational-observational method on a set of one hundred diverse funerals at the crematorium in Kremnička (Banská Bystrica), Slovakia, expands the sample in terms of:

- The number of officiants: religious and civil speakers
- Quantity: a sample of one hundred sermons and funeral addresses

---

27. Masarik, *Analýza nekérygmatických komponentov pohrebných*, 160.

- Variety of approaches: since I have included both civil and church funerals in the research. The church funerals include all the churches and religious groups that at the time of the research conducted a funeral service.

At the time of completing this work, only the participational-empirical observation of the services with the associated sound recording had been conducted. As I did not have this research registered as a scientific task, the precise processing of the obtained samples were suspended, but I will continue the research in the future.

A benefit of these observations for this work is that some of my observations I have reformulated as questions and working hypotheses which are reflected in the text of this work.

Synthesis

The synthetic approach represents the third phase of this study. In this phase, I search for the answers to the questions which arose in the previous analytical phases in combination with an attempt to take into account the wider theological discourse. In this way, I am trying to address the problems which arose in the analytical section, and my answers can be included in a comprehensive system which represents my contribution to the development of situational homiletics.

1

Definitions, Theological Justification, and Typological Specifics of Funeral Sermons

The Definition of a Funeral Sermon

The first part of this chapter will be devoted to (1) a number of definitions of funeral sermons which will include both Slovak and international versions; (2) attempting to choose the defining characteristics from the selected descriptions of funeral sermons; and (3) an attempt to form my own definition.

Existing Definitions of Funeral Sermons

Ján Jaminický uses the following definition of a funeral sermon: "A funeral sermon is a sermon in which the church at the burial of the deceased gives a living testimony about what they confess and believe about this earthly life and life in eternity, and . . . its task is through its own Christian testimony to directly prepare for the reality of the burial."[1]

Kunz defines a funeral sermon as the following: "A funeral sermon is an address directed to the listeners, which clarifies what the Christian faith means at the graveside for self-understanding and to allow people living today to understand the world."[2] According to Stebler, "funeral sermons can be in

---

1. J. Jamnický, *Evanjelické pohrebné kázne*, 98.
2. R. Kunz, *Die Auferweckung des Gekreuzigten als Thema der Grabrede*, 68. Cited in Ch. Stebler, *Die drei Dimensionen*, 50.

summary described as being rooted in the reformed tradition, theologically legitimate and a meaningful custom which takes the gospel message to beyond the church audience."[3]

Choosing the Defining Characteristics from the Existing Descriptions

Based on Filo's understanding of a funeral sermon,[4] we can derive the following observations for our definition:

1. Typological classification: "It is in fact a sermon."

2. Homiletical situation: "The threat of death to a life saved by Christ and the separation of those who belonged together."

3. The emphasized content: "A message about the victory of life over death in Jesus Christ, right at the moment when because of death there must be a parting with someone who believed in Christ."

4. The unique value of the message: "All other comfort fades in intensity and value before the comfort found in the salvation through God's son Jesus Christ. From the perspective of those saved for eternal life the finality of death and the farewell recedes."[5]

The theoretical discussion of funeral sermons by Igor Kišš contains the following points:[6]

1. Theological concept: Every funeral sermon must be Trinitarian.[7]

---

3. Ch. Stebler, *Die drei Dimensionen*, 34.

4. J. Filo, *Evanjeliové možnosti a problematika pohrebnej kázne*, in J. Filo, st, *Pohľady do neba. Kázne, príhovory a rozlúčky pri pohreboch a pietnych príležitostiach* (Vydavateľstvo Michala Vaška, Prešov, 2004), 278.

5. J. Filo, *Evanjeliové možnosti*, in J. Filo, *Pohľady do neba*, 279. Similar observations about early Christian funeral sermons are also offered by John Allyn Melloh, "Homily or Eulogy? The Dilemma of Funeral Preaching," *Worship* 67, no. 6 (N 1993): 515: "An important shift occurred when the classical model was adapted for Christian usage. Although the classical structure and *topoi* remained the same, the Christian faith, especially resurrection hope, furnished an 'incomparably superior means of consolation.' (But 'consolation' was based on doctrinal exposition.)"

6. I. Kišš, *Nádej nad hrobom*, 1.–4. časť, 2–4.

7. Ibid., 2: Every funeral sermon must be trinitarian in character. It can't just be a general proclamation of the gospel (the redemptive aspect of the sermon). It must contain something from the life of the deceased (the creative aspect), though without it becoming anthropocentric. The sanctifying aspect is then present when the minister places something from the life of the deceased as an example for believers, when it was observable that the deceased was being used by the Holy Spirit if he was a believer. The sanctifying character of the sermon can also be that sometimes things that are necessary to rebuke are indirectly talked about (in this it is never

2. Emphasized content: In a section of the sermon, there should be "the relationship between eternal life and a hope the overcomes the grave," and the conclusion should "offer comfort to the family."

3. The relationship between the case of the deceased and the message: "Every funeral sermon has to be above all else a sermon based on the Word of God and not the curriculum vitae of the deceased or an exaltation of them."

Sheppy understands a Christian funeral as "a remembrance of this person's death set in the framework of the Easter event."[8] This also fits with Jenssen's understanding of the funeral sermon as "pastoral proclamation."[9]

My Definition of a Funeral Sermon

When attempting to create a definition or name the characteristics of a funeral sermon, it is necessary to take into consideration the following viewpoints: (1) its essence; (2) the homiletical situation, which is the condition for its existence; (3) the subject who conducts it; (4) the purpose; and (5) the formal aspect. On the basis of these viewpoints, we can reach the following definition:

1. Essence. The essence of a funeral sermon is the proclamation of God's Word. It brings the message of God's grace in Christ, his victory over death and eternal life.

2. Homiletical situation. The situation of the listener who has been affected by the death of the deceased person and the impact of this on the religious and social experience of those present.

3. Subject who conducts it. It is preached by a minister who acts as a servant and representative of a specific Christian church.

---

mentioned that it applied to the deceased). A funeral sermon which talks generally about the message of the gospel of redemption in Christ and neglects the creative aspect (the life of the deceased) and the santifying aspect (lifting up the fruits of the Holy Spirit and rebuking the acts of the flesh) does not meet the objectives of a Christian funeral sermon.

8. P. Sheppy, *Death Liturgy and Ritual*, vol. 1, 8: "The Christian funeral is primarily a remembrance of this person's death set in the framework of the Easter event. It is not our hope that Uncle Fred was on balance a decent enough old chap – a bit of a rogue, but with a heart of gold – whom God will be delighted to have staying in the heavenly Hilton. Our hope is the salvation made possible, not by our human accounting system of good and bad, but by the grace of God manifest in raising Christ from the dead."

9. H. H. Jenssen, *Die Kirchliche Handlungen*, in *Handbuch der Praktischen Theologie*, vol. 2, 178.

4. Purpose. In order that those present are provided with pastoral support and a missionary opportunity.

5. Formal aspect. Using formally structured ecclesiastical language, which is a part of the church funeral rite.

Theological Justification of Funeral Sermons

Stebler gives four points that provide a theological justification of funeral sermons which I will present briefly here:[10]

1. Jesus, according to the Gospels, "didn't allow death the final word when he met with the deceased but with his complete power he transformed the situation be it on a death bed, bier or in the tomb." He brings new life to situations darkened by death.

2. The church has a commission to proclaim the gospel in season and out of season (2 Tim 4:2).

3. The church has in its declarations about the resurrection of Christ a matchless message when face to face with the phenomenon of death. The key statement of the Christian creed relates to overcoming death which is paradigmatically anticipated in Christ's death and resurrection.

4. The funeral sermon is also a possibility to personally address the bereaved in their specific life situation, and this in part is a demonstration of loving your neighbour in practice.

Stebler's reasons I regard as fully acceptable, but for the theological justification of funeral sermons, we should supplement them with the following emphases:

1. The eschatological perspective already determines the attitude of a Christian to life; therefore, in the moment of their departing, we need to continue with eschatology.

2. The minister becomes an instrument of God, who speaks to those present: the transcendental dimension of the event.

To Stebler's points 2 and 3, proclaiming the gospel and confessing Christ's resurrection, I wish to note that a funeral sermon is theologically legitimate

---

10. Ch. Stebler, *Die drei Dimensionen*, 32.

when the minister is consciously open to becoming an instrument proclaiming God's Word. In relation to proclamation, this raises the question about whether we are bringing God's Word or only human words about God. The bereaved who are overwhelmed by their loss could feel this shift as a burden. It is crucial that the minister brings the gospel because the bereaved are not required to listen to his personal opinions. For the theological justification of funeral sermons, this brings us to the conclusion that funeral sermons have a theologically legitimate place in a funeral only when in the moment of loss, they become an instrument proclaiming God's Word.

Typological Specifications of Funeral Sermons

If we were being very precise in our terminology, we would call a funeral sermon an ecclesiastical address which is set within the liturgy of a Christian funeral rite. But if it is called "a funeral sermon," we then need to simultaneously obtain more information which specifies its typological classification: (1) the typological characteristics of funeral sermons in order to be able to say if it is a sermon like all others or if it is a specific form of Christian sermon; (2) typological divisions of funeral sermons within Christianity; and (3) similar phenomena outside Christianity.

Typological Characteristics of Funeral Sermons

Filo states that a church funeral address is "a sermon on God's Word with everything that belongs to that as far as content and format is concerned."[11] I can identify with this statement because this classification of funeral sermons is supported by (1) general sermon characteristics, which all forms of preaching God's Word have in common as well as (2) specific sermon characteristics arising from the particular homiletical situation of a funeral.

General sermon characteristics of funeral sermons
Every sermon is a proclamation of God's Word to the life of its listeners. This proclamation must be based on a foundation of a thorough study of the sermon text (exegesis) and an inference of an applicable message to the specific homiletical situation of today's listeners (homiletical meditation). When doing this, the minister takes into consideration various perspectives,

---

11. J. Filo, *Evanjeliové možnosti*, in Filo, *Pohľady do neba*, 276.

from terminology to taking into account the listeners' problems and difficulties through to their objections and doubts. A sermon, and also a funeral sermon, aims to fulfil its homiletical objectives, and to achieve them it uses different tools. Its homiletical objectives correspond to its formal structure and its confessional anchoring in the theological positions of the church to which the minister belongs.

All of these statements refer not only to sermons which are part of a church service (or Roman Catholic homily), but also to funeral sermons. Josef Smolík's view is that it should be possible to include the funeral rite in the Sunday church service, and the existing practices, which have excluded it from the Sunday church service, are based more on technical rather than principled considerations.[12]

Specific sermon characteristics of funeral sermons

Although it is stated above that funeral sermons should have a whole array of characteristics meaning they are classed as sermons, we also discover that a set of other characteristics means they are a distinctive part of a minister's task of proclamation. These characteristics come to the fore if we compare factors such as the time, location, state of those present, etc., between a regular church service and a funeral. (See chart on page 17.)

One of the most significant distinctive features of a funeral sermon is the fact that it is the proclamation of God's Word into the situation of death, which is usually burdened by (1) loss, which causes a serious crisis in the personal lives of those affected; (2) the significantly altered psychological state of those present; and (3) a coming to terms with mortality and basic philosophical questions even for those who are emotionally uninvolved.

A noticeable difficulty of funeral sermons arises from the burdens which we can observe for both the minister and the listeners:

1. Difficulties for the minister. Smolík comments that the situation is characterized by death in which a person is at a loss for words.[13]

2. Difficulties for the listeners. The grief that the closest relatives are coming to terms with and the protective consequences of shock may

---

12. J. Smolík, *Radost ze slova*, 148. Smolík states that "Besides gathering around the word and the sacraments, there are also church services conducted for a variety of occasions. Occasions (weddings, funerals) could be included in the Sunday church service. That this is not taking place owes more to technical rather than principled considerations."

13. J. Smolík, *Radost ze slova*, 150.

mean that they have a considerably reduced ability to perceive the message which the minister specifically wants to address to them.

	Regular Church Service	Funeral
Time	Regular	Unplanned
Location	Church service meeting place Sermon topics unlimited	Crematorium evokes a limited range of topical areas connected to the loss of a loved one.[14]
Reason for gathering	Christians come in order to hear the proclamation of the Word and to fellowship with the believing community.	Secular people are not expecting a "message" from the minister. They expect that they will be enabled to have a dignified parting with the deceased. Believers are looking for help from God.
State of those present	The majority: normal everyday feelings of life.	The majority: disturbed by death and loss, shocked, grieving (but there may be some who are uninvolved in attendance).
Range of preaching and homiletical objectives	A reaction to all possible stimuli from life in the light of the Bible.	Limited topical range as well as methods of working with the biblical text.

Conclusion

In the section on the general characteristics of sermons, it was noted that funeral sermons can be typological classified as sermons (homilies) of the Christian church. But when taking into consideration the specific sermon characteristics, it can be affirmed that, although the funeral sermon is a part of the homiletical work of a minister, it forms a special category. A distinctive understanding of funeral sermons we can also note from Michalko, when on one hand he understands the funeral sermon as a sermon, but on the other hand he shows that to assess it, it is necessary to use specific criteria: "funeral sermons bring the message of God's Word but this is largely determined by

---

14. A funeral does not always have to take place in a crematorium.

the occasion. Therefore, evaluation of these sermons requires different criteria to that used with church service sermons."[15]

Further Classification of Christian Funeral Sermons

The above comments about general and specific characteristics of funeral sermons support their classification among the homiletical tasks of a minister. Funeral sermons themselves, though, are not a uniform phenomenon. When searching for the types, we can discover that, as in the past, so also today there exists a wide range of approaches. To illustrate this variability in approach, I have chosen the following examples: (1) references to the oldest accounts of Christian funeral sermons and their homiletical character; (2) types of funeral addresses from the period of Rationalism as presented by Jamnický; and (3) observations about the typological classification of funeral sermons in the Lutheran Church of the Augsburg Confession in Slovakia during the twentieth century and currently.

First, I will mention the oldest references to Christian funerals and their homiletical character. According to Stebler, the oldest references which we are aware of, "come from the fourth century from Gregory of Nazianzus, Gregory of Nyssa, John Chrysostom and Ambrose." At the same time, Stebler states that they were not yet funeral sermons but "lightly Christianised, highly standardized eulogies about the dead person." In this they stand in the ancient tradition of *laudatio funebris*.[16]

In a similar spirit, Jenssen states: "Already in the early church there were rare cases of sermons linked to the memory of a deceased person, similarly during the Reformation but having a separate funeral sermon only began in the middle of the sixteenth century."[17] At the same time, he maintains that during the Reformation, "they restricted themselves to objective sermons; rebuke or personal memories (*Gedächtnis*) were know only for exceptional figures. It was not until a later orthodoxy and above all Pietism and Rationalism that a space

---

15. J. Michalko, *Kázňové smery* (Liptovský Mikuláš: Tranoscius v Cirkevnom nakladateľstve Bratislava, 1955), 6.

16. Ch. Stebler, *Die drei Dimensionen*, 31. For information about the actual *laudatio funebris,* see Wilhelm Kiedorf, *Laudatio funebris: Interpretationen und Untersuchungen zur Entwicklung der römischen Leichenrede* (Beiträge zur Klassischen Philologie 106. Meisenheim a. Glan: Hain, 1980), 176.

17. H. H. Jenssen, *Die kirchliche Handlungen*, in *Handbuch der Praktischen Theologie, vol. 2*, 179.

was created for the remembrance of the deceased, but that should not prevent us from recognizing that this remembrance is theologically well grounded."[18]

The next example is from the period of Rationalism. Based on the characteristics of Jaminocký, which will be introduced later, we can discuss the following four types: (1) *sermo*; (2) *parentácia*; (3) address in front of the altar (*Standrede*); and (4) funeral sermon (*Leichenpredigt*).

1. *Sermo.* The minister speaks briefly and freely about utterances or thoughts which evoke the deceased. This approach is according to Jaminocký more religious-educational,[19] and based on my evaluation it does not possess the basic characteristics of a Christian funeral sermon.

2. *Parentácia.* It was based on the good attributes of the deceased, and according to Jaminocký, the text should have been based on a passage of Scripture, an utterance of the deceased, or a thought of his friends.[20] Here the biblical text is in a secondary position which in my point of view is unacceptable, as merely a source of inspiration and not as the Word which we listen to even when we are at a loss for words.

3. Address in front of the altar (*Standrede*). This, according to Jaminocký, had the most significant connection to the objective rules of the monastic orders of the church, but how it relates to the individual must be evaluated more critically. "It requires the insertion of a 'life history' to make it more interesting."[21] My understanding is that we do not refer to the individual to make things more interesting, but in order to support the process of saying goodbye and so that the gospel is brought into the real situation of loss. For this reason, we cannot continue with this situational-homiletical approach.

---

18. Ibid., 183.

19. J. Jamnický, *Evanjelické pohrebné kázne*, 21: Address – short, wedding speech about some kind of utterance or thought which *die Leiche herbeiführt* is for instruction or to provide contentment *Trauergesellschaft.* . . . In this kind of address . . . it is possible to caution those present against all kinds of prejudices, follies, or superstitions related to the dead, exhort them to greater vigilance toward the sick and dying, and advise them about new methods of treatment (for example vaccination against smallpox). Allegedly when these words are said at the right time, they often elicit deep and long-lasting impressions.

20. Ibid., 22: "*Parentácie.* In this the good attributes of the deceased should be taken in account, how he behaved during his illness, his principles, the care he received, etc."

21. Ibid.

4. Funeral address (*Leichenpredigt*). This was focused on the "life history," a continuous reflection on the deceased and his life story. According to Jamincký, this creates the risk that these kinds of sermons become "sermons of lies."[22] As the focus has moved from theology to the particular case, this approach is viewed as inappropriate.

In the search for positive historical models of proclaiming the Word at funerals for the present day, none of these approaches are suitable. Criticism of historical models would offer little benefit to current practice if we did not gain some information relevant to the present day. This we can gain from what was critiqued as it can point to possible risks of funeral preaching which even today need to be avoided.

In the case of the first type (*sermo*), focus can be drawn to the inadequately constructed starting points and aims. God's Word must always remain as the starting point of preaching, and the aims of individual funeral sermons must relate to the preaching aims of the biblical text and the homiletical situation of the listeners. This is therefore why a funeral sermon cannot become a platform for an educational lecture, even if the content is of value to those present.

In the second type (*parentácia*), the same shift in the starting point is found. It is not unequivocally the biblical text, but in place of it there can be "an utterance of the deceased or a nice thought from their friends." These kinds of alternative starting points are unacceptable for funeral sermons. Non-biblical starting points are usable as non-kerygmatic components of the funeral sermon, as secondary material, but as a matter of principle they cannot be a substitute for the biblical text.

In the third type of address (address in front of the altar), the use of observations about the deceased should be critically assessed. It is an unsatisfactory explanation that it is necessary to take into consideration the specific homiletical situation, and reducing the aims of a funeral sermon to making a more interesting sermon is also deemed inadequate because people confronted with the reality of death need to see life, that of the deceased and

---

22. Ibid. "The so-called 'life history' forms the main part of a *Leichenpredigt*, a funeral address which requires continuous reflection on the deceased and his life story, from this it is said to be possible to see 'what can happen to a person when it is important for them to gain the favour of others.' Let's hope that these sermons don't become 'sermons of lies' (*Lügenrede*). If there is anything good to say, it is necessary to emphasis a general truth and in this make the death instructive and educational for the living (Uhlhorn, 27–28)."

their own, from a theological-anthropological perspective – life under grace and with responsibilities before God.

Even the last mentioned type (funeral address), which overemphasizes the "case" by making it its starting point, does not proclaim God's Word. The shift of the starting point, if it becomes the "case" rather than the Bible, means the loss of the ability to speak the truth and exposes us to the risk that something that is not true will be said about the deceased. This brings the credibility of the minister into doubt.

An important part of these examples is also the twentieth century to the present day. In the Slovak Lutheran context, there has been for a long period of time a certain terminological searching,[23] which three professors of practical theology, Jamnický, Michalko, and Filo, have critically pointed out.

Jamincký quotes Harmas, whose writing differentiates between a "funeral address" and a "funeral sermon," yet both of these addresses are a part of the activity of the same minister at the same funeral.[24] Jamnický does not regard this differentiation as justifiable, and I share his opinion.

Michalko also observes a problem with the typological classification of funeral sermons, which is reflected in the terminology of Slovak Lutherans in the 1950s. On the one hand they are categorized as "situational addresses" along with baptismal, confessional, conformational, and wedding sermons, but he notes that "except for funerals, the others are named in church practice by the term 'address' or 'oration' which expresses their significant difference in character from a sermon."[25] At the same time, though, it is a matter for consideration if it is objectively justified to understand wedding and funeral sermons from the point of view of their typological classification as different categories, when they have a whole set of common homiletical characteristics and various domestic[26] and foreign works deal with them in joint chapters or in joint monographs.[27]

---

23. The terminological variation in the German environment is demonstrated by Ch. Stebler, *Die drei Dimensionen,* 18, where he states that the talk in the context of a church rite "is named as a sermon or an address."

24. J. Jamnický, *Evanjelické pohrebné kázne,* 76.

25. Michalko, *Kázňové smery,* 6.

26. P. O. Axman, and P. Aleš, *Homiletika,* 143. Situational preaching is covered on 82–86.

27. For example S. Rummage, "Redemptive Sermons." Similarly A. Malphurs and K. Willhite, eds. *Contemporary Handbook*; and W. Carr, *Brief Encounters.* The Roman Catholic church in Slovakia, for example Dr Jurko, publishes aids for the preparation of funeral and wedding sermons, with which he also expressed the typological similarity of these situational addresses.

The expression "funeral oration," which could indicate a separate category of homiletical activity, is also according to Filo problematic, because the address which the minister delivers at the funeral he regards as a "sermon with all that goes with it." The question of the typological classification of Christian funeral addresses he deals with by referring to the context in which it takes place (i.e. a church service) and to the specific characteristics of that address. After he states that this address is a sermon, he makes the second step which is to clarify that this sermon is in many parameters different to a usual church service sermon.[28] This is the same conclusion I reached above in the comparison of a number of characteristics of regular church service sermons and funeral sermons.[29]

In a Roman Catholic setting, the terms "homily" and "sermon" are used. A homily is the proclamation of a message based on a precisely defined text and is based on exegesis of the passage. A sermon, on the other hand, can be topical (i.e. without a strict link to a pericope). Therefore, it is a manifestation of the consistency of Roman Catholic authors that they use the expression "funeral homily" for the structure Protestant authors term funeral sermons.[30]

Other Types of Funeral Addresses

The aforementioned differences demonstrate that there are many possible approaches to what is said next to the coffin. This means that the current Christian funeral sermon is not a historically isolated phenomenon. Before and alongside the funeral sermon there existed and continues to exist other forms of funeral addresses which are based on religious or non-religious starting points. Currently, alongside funeral sermons there are (1) eulogies and (2) civil speeches.

Eulogies

The term "eulogy" is a compound word in the original Greek. The stem is *logos* (word), and it has the prefix *eu* (good). It is therefore "a good word" about the deceased which becomes the starting point and the primary emphasis of the address. This approach is found in both non-religious and religious (Christian) contexts, although I would deny the theological legitimacy of its occurrence in Christianity. This is why the eulogy is classified among parallel forms which are

---

28. J. Filo, *Evanjeliové možnosti*, in Filo, *Pohľady do neba*, 276.

29. See *Typological Characteristics of Funeral Sermons* above.

30. For example, Ľ. Stanček, *Pohrebné homílie* (Spišská Kapitula – Spišské Podhradie: Kňazský seminár biskupa Jána Vojtaššáka, 2003).

not identical to sermons. As Christian sermons always take the Bible as their starting point and not the deceased, we cannot consider a eulogy to be a valid alternative to preaching the Word, nor is it a theologically legitimate alternative. Reference to the deceased in funeral sermons is a separate phenomenon that needs attention. Its occurrence in a funeral sermon does not automatically mean that the emphasis is placed on it and that the funeral sermon has changed its character and become a eulogy. A eulogy is not built on religious ideas. It focuses on the personality of the deceased, and currently it represents one form of civil funeral address.

Civil funeral speeches

A civil funeral speech is a part of the funeral rite in which a non-religious community comes to terms with the death of a loved one. The range of themes includes the loss caused by the death of the deceased and the deceased's character, works, benefit to society, etc. The loss is come to terms with either on the basis of understanding death as a fact of life that a person must accept with dignity or on the basis of a wide range of philosophical starting points.

In the set of civil speeches I studied, I found some that were not written on the basis of an atheistic starting point. They contained a number of characteristics indicating religious awareness, but the inclusion of these characteristics is not to such an extent that they form the primary starting point. Therefore, they do not become religious speeches.

Certain forms of civil speeches do not allow space for a focus on the deceased as an individual. This occurs in the case of joint ceremonies after air disasters, traffic accidents, or industrial accidents, after which individual funerals are held. In the last few years there have been a number of such incidents in Slovakia.

2

The Homiletical Situation
of a Funeral

A requirement for the preparation of any sermon is not only the message of God's Word, but also knowledge about the situation within which it will be proclaimed. I understand the phrase "homiletical situation" as the extensive set of characteristics which describe the situation and without which it is impossible to fulfil the foundational homiletical requirement of proclaiming the Word of God into the situation of the listeners.[1] Characterizing the homiletical situation is therefore an objective necessity. We cannot afford to have doubts about it, even though in practice it is repeatedly overlooked. After all, ministers cannot preach without genuinely taking into consideration the context and cannot base it on invalid, unreal assumptions about the listeners of the sermon. They must always connect to the current state of the people with whom they are working.

The Terms "Differentiation" and "the Homiletical Situation"

In order to map all the important factors which adequately characterize the homiletical situation, I analyzed the data that Igor Kišš provides to characterize individual cases in his collection of sermons.[2] This data which he presents in

---

1. W. Carr argues that it is essential to take into consideration the homiletical context: "Indeed, one of the continuing themes of this essay is the way in which content and context may be too quickly separated in order to escape problems which have to be faced for effective ministry. If a problem is avoided, the chances are that an opportunity will also be missed. Context and content interact." *Brief Encounters*, 2.

2. See A. Masarik, *Analýza nekérygmatických komponentov pohrebných.*

the heading of each sermon under the title "differentiation"[3] covers three areas: (1) information about the deceased;[4] (2) the bereaved;[5] and (3) the church year. On the basis of a comprehensive evaluation of all the information in the analyzed sample,[6] I came to the conclusion that the majority of the information refers to the deceased. But the homiletical situation as understood by homiletics is predominantly defined by the listeners.

During later evaluation of the relationship between his differentiation and the wording of his funeral sermons, I came to the conclusion that Professor Igor Kišš in many places in his funeral sermons relies on a greater amount of homiletically relevant information than what is given in the differentiation. His information comes from a thorough knowledge of the family life, as well as the spiritual life, of the deceased person, or if need be from the composition of the funeral congregation and their needs. But in the differentiation, these categories are not included. This is why I came to the conclusion that the information which is stated under the summary title of "differentiation" does not report all the essential factors that a minister must take into account when preparing a sermon.

This summary of differentiation is a well-organized, simplified set of fundamental characteristics which specify the case, especially with respect to the deceased; but for the preparation of a sermon, we cannot regard it as an adequate consideration all the facets of the preaching context. Limiting oneself only to the characteristics of the "case," information about the deceased person could lead to overlooking other essential characteristics and weakening the ministry of the minister at the funeral. Therefore, it is necessary to search for a comprehensive theoretical definition of the factors that define the homiletical situation of the funeral.

---

3. The term "differentiation" describes in situational homiletics the specific characteristics of the individual case.

4. For example: "Lonely elderly gentlemen, devout."

5. In Kišš's differentiation, little consideration is given to the bereaved. Due to the infrequency of the occurrence of this criterion, when I originally prepared the work *Analýze nekérygmatických komponentov pohrebných kázní prof. Igora Kišša* (Banská Bystrica: PF UMB, 2008), I wanted to include it in chapter 1.6. But due to its importance, in the end I included it as a separate category so that ministers would think about the situation of the bereaved when differentiating the situation, and so that based on these observations, they would then search for an appropriate text for the sermon.

6. A. Masarik, *Analýza nekérygmatických komponentov pohrebných.* An analysis of the differentiation is found on 15–27.

Questions and Stimuli for Determining the Homiletical Situation

A number of authors have produced sets of questions or stimuli which can help ministers identify the homiletical situation of the funeral. Examples are (1) a set of questions from John Allyn Melloh; (2) a set of questions from Judith Wray; and (3) a set of stimuli from J. Filo Jr.

Question to Determine the Homiletical Situation from John Allyn Melloh

Melloh attempts to define the homiletical situation of those attending the funeral with the aid of the following questions.[7]

1. *What is the "emotion" that surrounds this celebration?* "A commonly shared feeling, even if negative, needs to be identified specifically. More importantly, however, the preacher should name the deeper and more permanently abiding 'affection' below the emotional surface."

2. *What has shaped this attitude?* Examples from Melloh include:
   - A sense of relief that long, painful suffering has ended may give rise to thankfulness.
   - Joy may be the attitude: a peaceful death brought someone at a ripe old age to an end.
   - The tragedy of an early or violent death may surface anger.

3. *How does the liturgy and the proclaimed Word speak to the event and to the attitude?* He gives as an example that God's Word may confirm our attitude, but it may challenge or even repudiate it.

4. *What new relationship between God and God's people obtains through this celebration?* An example he gives is that God's Word in the face of a tragedy may call us to solidarity and corporate hope.

The thought process that these questions follow does not relate only to defining the state of the bereaved and the others present, but also allows reflection about the church service.

---

7. J. A. Melloh, "Homily or Eulogy?," 518.

Question to Determine the Homiletical Situation from Judith Wray

Wray recommends asking the following questions.[8]

1. Who are the people who will hear this funeral sermon? Will they be family, friends, or business associates?

2. Are they here because they want to be or because they have to be?

3. How did the family relate to this person when alive?

4. Was the death expected or unexpected?

5. Were tragic circumstances involved?

6. What grief stages are the survivors currently in?

7. Who is being left out – absent children, ex-spouses, or lovers?

8. What is not being talked about – cancer, AIDS, suicide, a will, money, or unresolved disputes?

9. What is the faith commitment of these people in relation to that of the deceased?

What beliefs about life and death do the family and friends of the deceased cling to?

Stimuli to Determine the Homiletical Situation according to J. Filo

Filo states that "to correctly manage the preparation for a funeral sermon, we need to realize the situation in which the deceased passed away, many facts from his life and the situation of the bereaved in relation to the deceased."[9] With this in mind, he names the following categories:

1. The situation in which the deceased passed away

2. Information about the life of the bereaved

3. The situation of the bereaved in relation to the deceased.

---

8. J. H. Wray, "Preaching Life in the Face of Death," *Living Pulpit* 4, no. 3 (Jl–S 1995): 40.
9. J. Filo, *Evanjeliové možnosti*, in J. Filo, *Pohľady do neba*, 280.

Facets of the Homiletical Situation

On the basis of the summarized observations from my own research and the aforementioned stimuli from the academic discussion, I have reached the conclusion that the homiletical situation is determined by the following factors: the deceased, the funeral congregation, and the cultural context as well as other factors. As the funeral congregation, on the basis of relationships and emotional involvement, can normally be divided into the bereaved and the wider funeral congregation, we are left with the following spheres for defining the homiletical situation: (1) the deceased; (2) the bereaved; (3) the wider funeral congregation; (4) ministers; (5) the cultural and religious context; and (6) other factors – church year, etc.

The Deceased Person

Keith Willhite begins his notes about the funerals he has conducted with the range of cases into which he has come into contact: "I have conducted funerals for children, suicide victims, accident victims, people who have never darkened the door of a church, and devout believers."[10] This diversity leads us to the issue of the defining characteristics which a minister must be aware of for the specific case of the deceased. On analyzing the differentiation,[11] it is possible to observe the following set of seven factors, some of which the minister must regularly take into consideration and others only occasionally: gender; age; spirituality; relationships; health; manner of death; and other notes.[12]

Gender

The deceased's gender is an important influence which is not negated by the equality of men and women. There is, of course, also the need to use the appropriate grammar when referring to the deceased.

---

10. K. Willhite,"Introduction," Part Two, Funerals, in *Contemporary*, eds. A. Malphurs and K. Willhite, 149.

11. A. Masarik, *Analýza nekérygmatických komponentov pohrebných*, 15–27.

12. In connection with the deceased, Wray asks the following questions: "Who is this person who has died? Was the deceased young, old? Is there a significant other? Was the person married? How many times? Are there children, parents, siblings? What do you know of the person's social status, work experience, faith testimony, struggles, successes, failures? What key word or image do people associate with this person? What beliefs about life and death did the deceased have?" "Preaching Life in the Face of Death," 40.

Age of the deceased

The age of the deceased is an important parameter, but the minister does not need to have it precisely defined, as it is enough to know the approximate age category of the deceased. An exception would be if the deceased had just reached or nearly reached an important jubilee anniversary.

Spirituality of the deceased

I understand the phrase "spirituality of the deceased" to mean the faith, devotion, Christian life, and worldview of the deceased. A church funeral talks about a person before God. This is why for a Christian funeral, the spirituality of the deceased is one of the most important questions. In spite of all the risks which are associated with overestimating or underestimating the spirituality of the person we have to bury, I believe that this information is of great importance for the minister, even in cases when in the final wording of the funeral sermon it is not used. In this sense, the most important thing is not whether this information was or was not formally included in the differentiation, but the key is whether ministers when remembering the deceased (if they knew the person) or when asking questions about the deceased (if they did not know the person), pay attention to this aspect and theologically evaluate the importance of their observations when preparing the funeral sermon.

Categories of observations about the spiritual life

There are different ways of categorizing our notes about the spiritual life of the deceased. Two systems of categorizing will be cited here: (1) from Ján Jamnický; and (2) from the results of my analysis of the homiletical differentiation.

Jamnický distinguished four categories of deceased:[13]

1. Diligent Christians. He did not want to use the expression "perfect" Christians.

2. Mundane, formal Christians: "About whom it is not possible to find either a particular degree of devotion or a lack of it – in the world there are many Christians of this type."

3. People whose character is called into question.

4. Those in bondage to sin.

His view of the homiletical connection to each category is as follows:

---

13. J. Jamnický, *Evanjelické pohrebné kázne*, 83.

1. In the case of diligent Christians, "it is necessary to stress and bring to the forefront God's grace and not human achievements; the good the person manifested in the terms of thoughts, feelings and words and proved in deeds, needs to be credited to God's grace rather than the person."[14] So the minister should proceed in such a manner that the deceased is not exalted but that gratitude is expressed to God. In this way, it is possible to move from the case of the deceased to the theological testimony.

2. In the case of mundane, formal Christians, Jamnický criticizes any embellishments in the evaluation of the deceased at the funeral, and he raises an interesting theological question when he asks, "whether in the interest of truth the minister is required . . . to demonstrate that this kind of life, in the light of the Scriptures, is shown to be a serious failing due to the unfulfilled requirement to live a positive Christian life?"[15]

3. In the case of the deceased whose character is called into question, Jamnický warns of the risks the minister can get into when he wants to "use pitiful fabrications to rescue . . . the honour of that person." According to Jamnický, a danger for the minister is that certain partial observations from the life of the deceased will be judged as signs of their spiritual life.[16]

4. The case of those in bondage to sin is the hardest for the minister, and here a large amount of pastoral wisdom and tact is required to not deny the truth, to not insult the bereaved, and to not provide fuel for gossips. In this case, Jamnický advises the minister to stick to "a choice of general objective ideas," or to stick to biblical emphases, and he adds Uhlhorn's advice to also demonstrate the responsibility of each individual for the sins of their neighbours.[17] With this Jamnický evidently wants to move from critical judgement of the case to thinking about everyone's responsibilities before God.

Categories based on the analysis of the differentiation

These observations were compiled by extracting references about the person which were hidden within Kiss's differentiation, then by dividing them into positive comments and negative comments, and finally classifying them.

---

14. Ibid., 84.
15. Ibid., 86.
16. Ibid., 88.
17. Ibid., 89.

(a) **Positive comments** about the spirituality of the deceased person can be expressed for example as signs of spiritual life;[18] the position in the church of the deceased;[19] the importance of the deceased for the local church;[20] Christian engagement in the world, etc. Naturally this is not a fixed list.

(b) **Negative comments** about the spirituality of the deceased person can be the opposite of what was mentioned as positive comments, for example, major expressions of a lack of any impact of spirituality on the personal life of the deceased, or problematical ethical attitudes and so on.[21]

This information is of great importance so that the minister can appropriately word references to the deceased – being respectful but without saying things which do not reflect the truth.

Relationships

The homiletical situation of the grieving family cannot be defined without consideration of their relationships with the deceased – not just the nature, but also the quality. Therefore, differentiations compiled without this information are only possible if ministers already know all their parishioners intimately and can take into consideration their relationships without formally making a list for the funeral sermon.

But if a realistic evaluation of the relationships is not taken into consideration, ministers do not know if they have in front of them a case of harmonious relationships, which is a reason to invite them to thankfulness to God for the gift they had in the deceased, or if it is the opposite case, where the bereaved must deal with anger towards the deceased and attempt to find a new way of being "freed" from the person. Naturally in this case it is not possible to

---

18. The spiritual life of the individual can be indicated by these types of comments: devoted to God's will, good Christian, a strong believer, a servant of the Lord, self-sacrificing, humble, obedient to God. For a man: lovingly served his family and church, believing. For a woman: mother; devout, Mary and Martha in one person, a wife whom God helped to overcome all difficulties in life, etc.

19. References to a position in the local church (churchwarden, young presbyter) can be but don't have to be a reflection of the spiritual life of the deceased. It would though be a huge mistake if on the other hand the minister overlooked this information because in normal circumstances, serving in the church is a very significant expression of the spirituality of the deceased.

20. For example: a pillar of the church. This includes a whole set of features that the minister should become aware of. People who enrich the church fellowship in any number of ways without being given a function are of great importance to the church community, and their work is an expression of their spiritual life.

21. I. Kišš stated in two cases the same negative comment "indifferent to religion." From the text of the funeral sermon, it was impossible to be more specific about what this comment actually meant in these particular cases. *Nádej nad hrobom*, 111, 135.

talk about thankfulness and intense sorrow, even though the process of coming to terms with the loss after complicated relationships is no easier. Therefore, I regard it as risky to use funeral sermons from a collection of sermons if they are chosen based only on basic information about the deceased person and as the next step the question of relationships is not considered. This kind of approach significantly limits the potential of the funeral sermon to fulfil its role.

When characterizing relationships, it is necessary to perceive both (a) positive comments as well as (b) negative comments in a sensitive way.

(a) Positive comments about the relationships of the deceased person are mainly first-hand testimonies about relationships. But there are also statements that are only possible to make where there were healthy relationships, and for that matter the deceased's relationships are expressed by care shown to different groups of people. First-hand testimonies about healthy interpersonal relationships are clearly understandable and do not need clarifying. They are an expression of a healthy personality and the person's appropriate integration into their social context.

Clues of healthy relationships. The minister needs to be sensitive to comments that indirectly demonstrate healthy relationships. For example, a comment that the deceased was "the patriarch of the family and a churchwarden" can mean that he was a socially healthy individual whose passing means a loss for those affected. A more concise expression of the same fact can be given by the comments such as: favourite elderly gentleman, pillar of the church, good wife and mother, good mother, loving mother, or the simple sigh with the words that the deceased "will be missed." Also, a testimony like, "the Lord helped her overcome all life's problems," can in the relevant theological context mean the deceased did not have an easy life. But if she overcame all her problems through faith in God, the pastor might conclude that this person was so formed by her faith in God, through her trials, that she became a person incapable of forming negative relationships. All of these comments refer to a relational richness which is lost following the departure of the deceased.

Expressions of relationships through care for different groups of people. When relationships are expressed through caring, we notice that some people are very attentive to a certain group, for example, family and church, whereas others are prepared to help whoever needs their help. For this reason, ministers who are starting out need to be warned that they should not automatically make generalizations even from such positive observations. If the individual had high quality relationships in one community, it does not necessarily mean that all that person's relationships were high quality. There is the problem of "group egoism" in which a person behaves differently in one defined group from others outside it – internally in the group the person is obliging, but outside the group the person behaves selfishly.

(b) Negative comments about the deceased person are observations about stressful realities which affected the life of the deceased and which will influence the bereaved during the funeral. For understandable reasons, only a few examples will be mentioned which should act as an impetus for ministers to learn more and will reveal the relationship between the problems observed and their impact on the course of the funeral. Such examples include: a lack of wisdom in parenting, egoism, alcoholism, the return of an unfaithful spouse, and gambling.

A lack of wisdom in parenting, or foolish love to one child. In practice, I have observed cases where a parent supported one adult child and demanded help from another. For one, parents had resources, and from the other they demanded. In the final analysis, it meant that one child was subsidized from the resources of the other. This behaviour is easy to detect, and it damages not only the relationships with the parent but also the relationships between the siblings. This is not to deny that there can be situations where solidarity between family members is necessary. But if it is to be an expression of healthy relationships, it requires transparency, and the one expected to provide help should be able to decide freely. If the family did not have enough strength to compensate for this negative influence, then they will not go to the funeral as a homogenous grieving community. One is grieving for a loving parent, and the other is grieving for a parent who didn't have a place for them in their heart. The same problem can also arise if there is favouritism in how the inheritance is divided.[22] If this outcome is already known about by the time of the funeral, then some of the bereaved are thinking more about the injustice and material loss, against their expectations, than about the relational loss. So in the place of grieving we meet with jealousy which can be connected to the relationship of another family member to the deceased as well as to how the inheritance is

---

22. It is sad to observe people who regularly attended church but did not have enough wisdom in their personal life to avoid putting a burden on the relationships of their heirs. In one specific case, the father before death orally gifted one daughter the same part of the estate as the mother orally gifted to the second. All the while, they didn't communicate with the other party. Even though legally these actions were unfounded, their daughters dragged the case through the courts for years.

to be shared, which opens the questions of how the deceased valued the one to whom they left less.[23]

Egotism. Individuals who do not care about their families, only about themselves, damage (abuse) their families and are able to manipulate them into feeling guilty. The minister must therefore anticipate that the bereaved will need help to come to terms with their memories of the quality of their relationships with the deceased, as well as coming to terms with the so-called "immature feelings of guilt" when they blame themselves for things they could not have done. If they have the ability to take a detached view, they will regard the deceased's death as a kind of liberation from manipulation and at the same time have feelings of guilt for this sense of liberation.

Alcoholism. The problems connected to alcoholism are well known in Slovakia. Apart from the serious financial problems it causes, it also has a negative impact on the family on many levels. For example, the alcoholic may create guilt in family members, there may be deep sadness or an inability to grieve, and in some cases also a feeling of relief at the death of the deceased.

Return of an unfaithful spouse. One of Kišš's differentiations reads: "unfaithful husband who left his family and before death returned to his first wife."[24] In this kind of case, ministers have before them a spouse who had been left and had to come to terms with the departure and after a time also had reaccepted that spouse. At the funeral service, the remaining spouse will have all of this in their mind. It is also possible that the deceased returned to their first spouse after a crisis in their new relationship or on the basis of another crisis situation which led them to revaluate their earlier departure. Therefore, it is questionable if the couple managed to enjoy a quality relationship on the spouse's return. If the remaining spouse idealizes the deceased, it will complicate their process of coming to terms with the loss – as all the deficiencies in their relationship will be viewed as being the remaining spouse's fault. In the place of the guilt of the unfaithful spouse, there can be unjustifiable feelings of guilt on the side of the bereaved, and maybe others close to the bereaved. The minister should not leave this kind of family without pastoral care.

Gambling. These may be people who gambled before their retirement and stole from their own home in order to have money for their addiction. For the family, this behaviour created a financial and relational situation that was unbearable. It led to the marriage being seriously damaged and the

23. See *Bereavement: Support When You Need It Most*, information sheet, "Grief within the Family" (Richmond: Cruse Bereavement Care, 2010).

24. I.Kišš, *Nádej nad hrobom 1*, 26.

children being embarrassed about their parent. If these kinds of people die at a time when they have debts on all sides, and their family is overwhelmed by their behaviour, then we can expect a set of varied feelings from sorrow to embarrassment or even anger at the funeral.

We need to note that information about the quality of the deceased's life and relationships is not collected for publication. The minister's role is not to inform about the deceased but to preach God's Word into the situation of loss. Therefore, ministers must consider with great sensitivity and make wise pastoral decisions about those aspects to reflect in the funeral sermon.

Health

Comments about the health of the deceased person are significant for defining the homiletical situation in two cases: when the deceased was healthy and the family were not prepared for the deceased's passing; and when different manifestations and degrees of illness influenced the life of the deceased and the family. It is possible to illustrate both groups with examples from my analysis of Kišš's funeral sermons.

The death of a healthy person. In this case, the minister establishes that the deceased was relatively healthy and the bereaved were taken by surprise. They didn't have any signals of danger or the need to prepare for the farewell. The unpreparedness does not have to relate only to their ability to process the loss, but also to the many unresolved relational or economic matters which may be difficult to resolve and therefore represent a separate set of serious problems.

Dependence on help. In situations where the deceased "in the end needed care from their children," the bereaved may be tired from giving care to the dependent person and internally had the chance to prepare for the farewell. They have undergone a period of being daily with that person, and sometimes had the opportunity to speak about important issues. However, we cannot overlook the fact that tiredness and the restlessness of the dying represent a separate stressful area. For the bereaved who were carers, this may be a subject of remorse despite their efforts to provide maximum help.

Degenerative changes caused by illness. In some cases, there is a rapid onset of degenerative changes affecting the person's health – sometimes only somatic but in others also psychological. In these situations, people's values and behaviour can change, and their areas of interest can shrink, resulting in a whole set of stressful changes. In a socially sensitive environment, these changes acted as a signal that the person's passing was near. On the other hand, these changes could have caused a worsening of relationships. Therefore, even a family who had enjoyed good times in the past may, due to these negative changes, have bad memories of their final days together.

Difficult course of a terminal illness. In this case, the family has endured an exhausting time of accompanying the dying person. Yet at the same time, they have behind them extensive preparation for processing their grief. They can be physically and spiritually exhausted, but they may still be taken by surprise if they had expected the death to come months or weeks later. They enter the post-death period of dealing with loss from a completely different starting point from those who lose a relative unexpectedly.

An impending serious illness. In this case, the family could to a certain extent come to terms with the impending illness and make preparations for a difficult time. They were afraid of the difficulties that awaited them. In place of the serious illness, they experienced what was expected at the end of a stressful time. This can be experienced in two ways: as the worst option, the deceased could have lived longer, or the best, at least the deceased did not have to suffer.

Gradual decline. In this situation, the bereaved had the chance to notice intuitively the signs that signalled that something was happening with their loved one. They could either process the question "What if I lose this person?" or run away from this question. They can have feelings of guilt that they neglected something or feelings of anger that the doctors neglected something. This group of people may have endured a long period of searching for medical or spiritual help and may have experienced a variety of responses to their searching.

Manner of death

The cause of death should be taken into consideration for the homiletical situation, along with the information about health, because it has the same significance for the state of the bereaved and their reaction to the death. The least prepared for loss are the bereaved who have to face a sudden death and dramatically experience a tragic death. Among the most difficult from the point of view of loss, as well as of frequency of occurrence, the most serious are tragic accidents, murder, and suicide. Some comments about the impact of the manner of death on the bereaved are included in the following section.

The Bereaved

In an analysis of a collection of Protestant funeral sermons, I came to the conclusion that when cases are being classified, information about the bereaved is not treated in an adequate manner, and the differentiation mainly contains information about the deceased. This observation can also be applied to the usual method of defining the case used by foreign authors. Funeral sermons available on the internet, based on the search term "funeral sermons," are normally classified by the case of the deceased, and they do not have any description of the homiletical situation. But the homiletical situation of a funeral, its context, is not only defined by the deceased but is especially defined by those who attend the funeral service within which the bereaved form the most important group. Therefore, it is necessary to pay considerable attention to them. Even though there are funerals where there are no close relatives and the deceased departs without anyone experiencing intensive grief, the majority of funerals are attended by close relatives and others who need to come to terms with the loss.

As a general statement, it can be affirmed that grieving is a universal human phenomenon which occurs in many forms throughout the whole of human society.[25] Its intensity in different cases of loss varies, meaning that we cannot approach every funeral as if it is a source of unbearable pain. There are very difficult farewells. But there are funerals where the level of pain is lower, and there are even cases where the bereaved are grateful that the suffering caused by illness is over.[26] But it does not mean they do not grieve. Sad cases are funerals where the family does not grieve for the deceased due to broken relationships.[27] The bereaved are not a homogenous group. The loss of a loved one affects them at different ages,[28] with differing qualities of relationship to

---

25. J. W. Worden: "There is evidence that all humans grieve a loss to one degree or another. Anthropologists who have studied other societies, their cultures, and their reactions to the loss of loved ones report that whatever the society studied in whatever part of the world, there is an almost universal attempt to regain the lost loved object, and/or there is the belief in an afterlife where one can rejoin the loved one." J. W. Worden, *Grief Counselling and Grief Therapy: A Handbook for the Mental Health Practitioner* (London: Tavistock Routledge, 1991), 9, quoted in P. Sheppy, *Death Liturgy and Ritual, vol. 1*, 44.

26. A man who for a long time and in an exemplary manner cared for his wife with cancer told me: "Now I am very ashamed, but I prayed for it all to end. Thanks be to God that it is over. I couldn't watch how she suffered."

27. A young man from a socially difficult environment recollected the funeral of his father with the words, "At his funeral, I didn't cry at all. I didn't like him and I didn't care."

28. Cruse Bereavement Care, *Bereavement Care in Practice: The Cruse Approach to Working with Bereaved People* (Richmond, UK: Cruse Bereavement Care, 2004), 72. For the purposes of support while grieving, children and young people are divided into the following groups: younger children (2–5 years old); children (5–10 years old); and adolescents (see 45–47). About children attending funerals, psychologists P. Donnelly and G. Connon state:

the deceased, and they have different psychological[29] and spiritual suppositions about dealing with loss.[30]

The intensity of grieving cannot be ascertained from external expressions of grieving while the minister is meeting with the bereaved or during the funeral. The fear that the bereaved have about whether they can bear the emotional burden of the funeral expresses itself in the way they concentrate on bearing it at the funeral. In other words, this means a reduction in external expressions of pain,[31] thus demonstrating greater self-control for cultural reasons. Apart from this, there are also psychological influences which affect the ability to grieve and express sadness.[32] From my own experience, I know a case where a bereaved man stated that "If I could only wail . . . but I can't. It's suffocating me!" An observer who attempted to estimate the dynamics of stress based only on external expressions would come to the conclusion that the man in question "didn't even cry."

Sometimes the bereaved do not present their loss as a loss of the relationship but as a loss of the benefits that the relationship brought them. When we hear declarations of an economic character such as "What will become of us?" "Who will pay for the flat and children's education?" we cannot automatically

---

Family and social rituals (e.g. funerals) allow both children and adults to come to terms with difficult situations, and should be encouraged. Families often try to protect children from these experiences, but children are much less likely than adults to be distressed in such circumstances. Many families have the tradition of viewing the body. This can be a sensitive issue, but children usually react better than adults as long as they are prepared for the experience. Viewing the body may or may not be advisable depending on the circumstances of death; funeral directors and religious representatives can offer good advice on such matters. *Guidelines for the Immediate Response to Children and Families in Traumatic Death Situations. Professionals Guide* (Belfast: The Royal Hospitals, 2003), 4.

29. Here it is necessary to take into consideration whether the person has a stable or unstable personality, whether they have experienced previous losses, and the level to which they have been dealt with.

30. Therefore, it is essential that situational homiletics is in a critical conversation with all scientific disciplines that can aid in understanding the homiletical situation of the bereaved.

31. I heard the opposite case from a civil celebrant, Šustek, at the crematorium in Banská Bystrica. A Roma widow stood up during the ceremony and fainted from grief. As he didn't want to interrupt the ceremony, Šustek asked the staff of the crematorium to call for medical assistance through the sound system. When the woman who had "fainted" heard this, she got up and sat back in her place.

32. J. Moltmann states, "The modern inability to grieve is probably also grounded in the media culture of the modern world. We note what we see on the television screen, but it hardly touches us. We see the world through the mirror of the media and don't know whether they are giving us a reflection of the real world or not. The secondary experiences communicated through the media overlie our primary existential experiences. What is authentic and what isn't? We can no longer distinguish. So did the Gulf War really take place in Iraq, or only on the CNN channel?" *In the End – the Beginning* (London: SMC, 2004), 122.

conclude that there is an inadequate relational side to the loss. These questions demonstrate that the bereaved are aware of the change in situation and how it will impact them in many ways.

In certain cases of socially pathological families, there can be an absence of grieving, or the bereaved may not be able to begin the grieving process due to conflicts in their relationships.

Dealing with grief

Dealing with loss has psychological stages, marks and tasks, which have been studied by authors such as Erich Lindemann,[33] Elisabeth Kübler-Ross, Colin Murray Parkes, and J. William Worden. The most widely known is the description of the stages of grief by Kübler-Ross,[34] though these stages are often mistakenly understood as a linear description of discrete stages that follow each other. It should not be forgotten that her phases are descriptive rather than normative, as all grieving is an expression of the individual, and the stages are contingent on the individual's personality.

According to Worden, the expression and course of grief, its progress, and final result are influenced by the following factors: (a) the character and depth of the relationship between the grieving and the deceased; (b) how the person died – as a result of natural causes, an accident, suicide, or murder; (c) how the grieving person generally deals with anxiety and stress; (d) the existence of previous experiences with grieving; (e) religious or cultural ties with the accompanying expectations for behaviour or support; and (f) the existence of other stress factors in the life of the grieving person other than grieving.[35]

These factors are important in determining the homiletical situation in relation to the bereaved, meaning not just the immediate situation at the funeral. Therefore, this structure of factors has been used to make certain observations.

(a) The character and depth of relationship between the grieving and the deceased. This factor includes first family relationships when the bereaved was a parent, marriage partner, child, sibling, etc. of the deceased. Different

---

33. E. Lindemann, "Symptomatology and Management of Acute Grief," in *American Journal of Psychiatry* 101: 141–148.

34. E. Kübler-Ross: *On Death and Dying: What the Dying Have to Teach Doctors, Nurses, Clergy and Their Own Families* (London and New York: Routledge, 2009). The stages are described as first stage: Denial and Isolation (31–39); second stage: Anger (40–65); third stage: Bargaining (66–68); forth stage: Depression (69–90); and fifth stage: Acceptance (91–111).

35. J. W. Worden, *Grief Counseling and Grief Therapy: A Handbook for the Mental Health Practitioner* (New York: Springer, 2009), n. 57.

levels of relationship create different areas of stress for each bereaved person. After the funeral, adult children who no longer live with their parents return to their professional and closer family lives. In contrast, widowed partners return to the empty flat where they are awaited by a long and intensive period of processing the loss. The second factor is the quality of the relationship, such as ambivalent, intense, dependent, or balanced.

By assigning these two criteria to each relative, it is possible to gain an approximate assessment of the differentiated stress. But the issue is much broader and more complicated – for example, Parkes observes that conflict in one or more areas of marriage complicates the grieving process.[36] Therefore, it is necessary to take into account the connection between the quality of the relationship and the grieving process. Based on today's divorce statistics and the overall crisis of the family, we can assume that this observation relates to a large proportion of marriages, and generally the bereaved must be to some degree facing this kind of complication.

Viliam Šustek, the late civil funeral celebrant at the crematorium in Banská Bystrica Slovakia, observed that the value structures of Slovak society have changed significantly. According to him, battles over the property of the deceased frequently cause conflict situations in the already emotionally charged atmosphere. He mentioned a case where the bereaved, because of the inheritance, quarrelled and even fought each other with umbrellas in the entrance hall of the crematorium. A family which is angry or fighting over the inheritance loses the potential for mutual support in the processing of the loss. Therefore, in this situation, the resultant stress factors must be considered.

(b) Manner of the death – the result of natural causes, accident, suicide or murder. Society's attitude to certain causes of death, for example suicide or a family murder, and certain illnesses, for example AIDS, can cause the bereaved to not receive the level of support they need to cope with the loss. These examples are included as stimuli for ministers in their assessment of factors that will influence the grieving process in a particular case.

Grieving for the very elderly. The estimation of the emotional burden on the bereaved cannot be based on schematic notions. Observations from a number of cases show that the quality of the relationship with the deceased, rather than age, is the decisive factor in determining the depth of the grief. Even when an elderly person leaves the family, it breaks relationship bonds, which causes

---

36. C. M. Parkes, *Bereavement: Studies of Grief in Adult Life,* first ed. 1972, 3rd ed. (Philadelphia: Taylor & Francis, 2001), 155.

great pain and sorrow. Frequently this pain is not possible to judge based on tear-stained faces but it is hidden in the hearts of the bereaved. Ministers who, at the passing of someone of advanced years, do not notice the pain of grief have not understood one of the tasks that their work should fulfil.

Grieving after a suicide. Those grieving after a suicide include deeply wounded relatives who have unspeakable pain, unanswerable questions, and feelings of guilt which they have not yet been able to sort into "true" and "false." A clearer indication of suicide's impact on the bereaved is given by the statement, "They estimate that for every person who takes their own life, six people suffer devastating grief."[37] The English support organization, Cruse Bereavement Care, states that this kind of bereavement may result in the following responses:[38]

- Confusion. The constant question "why?" will not be answered even if a suicide note is found. The bereaved only find out how the deceased felt at the time of committing suicide but not the full story.
- Guilt. The bereaved have many "if only" scenarios and think how they could have prevented the suicide from happening. Guilt can be the most destructive of emotions.[39] Suicide is rarely the result of a sudden impulse. What appears to be the reason may be just one contributing factor and the core reason much deeper.
- Shame and isolation. Suicide causes the bereaved to be socially stigmatized. So they feel isolated and without social support, and the duress from their surroundings means they are unable to grieve.
- Anger. The bereaved often have the feeling that the death could have been prevented. Anger may be directed towards the deceased or themselves or lead to family members blaming each other. There

---

37. Cruse Bereavement Care, *Bereavement Care in Practice* (Richmond: Cruse Bereavement Care, 2004), 21.

In the case of suicide, I recommend H. W. Robinson, J. E. Means, and P. D. Borden, "Guidelines for Difficult Funerals," in *A Contemporary Handbook for Weddings and Funerals and Other Occasions*, 212: "Suicides present a very difficult situation, regardless of whether the person is a believer. If you're going to touch on the fact that the person is a believer, you probably need to touch on the fact that all of us as believers do things wrong. Moreover, those who attend the funeral of a suicide victim are usually guilt stricken. We do not want to pile onto their guilt. It seems wise to avoid trying to explain a suicide."

38. Cruse Bereavement Care, *Bereavement: Support When You Need It Most*, thematic sheet, Death by Suicide (Richmond: Cruse Bereavement Care, 2013).

39. We can assume that when the bereaved are believers, this guilt will be present to an even greater degree as they experience both societal and religious guilt of being complicit in the sin of the deceased.

is a risk of irreversible damage to their relationships and to the fragmentation of family support. If there is a suicide which the family is able to conceal, they may later suffer as they process the repercussions of concealing it.

Grieving after a murder in the family. A murder in the family is an expression of a relationship crisis. If it was not a momentary impulse, there may have been relationships that have been damaged for a long time which culminated in murder.[40] The minister must expect emotional confusion in all the bereaved with expressions of regret or hatred. If the murder is proven and the suspect is convicted, any children in the family lose not only the murder victim but also the convicted person. Those who are grieving from the family of the guilty person, if they even come to the funeral, have an incredibly complicated position if they identify with the grieving and at the same time are regarded as supporting the guilty person. In summary, this is a situation which after the funeral requires extensive pastoral-psychological intervention focused on processing the loss and healing relationships.[41]

Grieving death from an unacceptable illness. Those grieving after a death from a socially unacceptable illness form a separate group. Due to the illness, for example AIDS, the patient as well as the relatives become socially isolated, and often they do not receive the help and support they need, even from the church. For them the funeral can mean grief, shame, and exclusion from relationships.

* * *

While I was in the USA in 1995, I had dinner with the parents of a deceased university student who contracted AIDS in a homosexual relationship. They told me how their son's illness had led them into isolation. So the parents, their son, and their family remained without social and spiritual

---

40. Jesus's statement in Mark 13:12–13, "And brother will deliver brother over to death, and the father his child, and children will rise against parents and have them put to death. And you will be hated by all for my name's sake. But the one who endures to the end will be saved." This demonstrates that internal family relationships will in the "end times" be marked by anger for religious reasons (see also Matt 10:21: "Brother will deliver brother over to death, and the father his child, and children will rise against parents and have them put to death"). In the case of a radicalized interreligious situation, the minister must take this possibility into account.

41. Life in hatred of your relatives – for example murderers – negatively impacts the later life of the bereaved. The minister cannot place forgiveness as the homiletical aim and force the bereaved to forgive. This kind of homiletical aim I regard as inappropriate. It can be set as a pastoral aim in the setting of long-term pastoral care, and gradually and sensitively they can be led to forgiveness.

support during the hardest period. They lost friends along with pastoral and relational support from the local church.

They dealt with the situation in an exemplary manner. Despite a conservative Christian disapproval of their son's homosexual past, they were able to remain loving to him. He also dealt with his past in a confessional conversation. With thankfulness to God for the certainty of the forgiveness of sins, he prepared for his death with his parents. During the terminal stage, the parents took turns to be by his hospital bed, and in the moment when he died, his father was quietly reciting from the psalms.

This case is one of the most striking examples of the ability to identify with a loved one in his failing, a responsible relationship to a relative, and simultaneously the processing of a crisis situation from a faith perspective. After processing their own life crisis, they were able to tend to patients with AIDS and their relatives, so that at least in their organization, they partially reduced the experience of being excluded from the community.

The same father recollected to me the case of a mother whose daughter had the same illness. The mother was prepared to bear the burden, but the burden in isolation was unbearable. Therefore, she screamed: "God! If only she had cancer! But she has AIDS!" In the case of cancer, she would have had social and spiritual help, but for this she was on her own.

During the same journey to the USA, I also visited a minister whose son – a haemophiliac – contracted AIDS from a blood transfusion. He recalled that during the time of caring for their dying son, they had extensive support from the church. One hall in the church building is even named in his memory.

These various examples demonstrate that the exclusion is probably caused by fear of danger in combination with condemnation as "guilty," and not the illness itself.

* * *

Grieving after social exclusion and non-adaption or homelessness. A young man from a normal Slovak family became homeless. His sister worked and was an external student at university. Her brother contacted her only for financial help, and she was unable to meet his requests. A number of times she tried to help him fit back into normal life, yet all her attempts ended unsuccessfully. Finally, her brother died, and it took her a long time to deal with the difficult feelings of guilt even though she was not responsible for his situation and had done what she could to help. Frequently it was outside her personal capabilities. His death also created feelings of shame in her and her family despite not being personally responsible for it.

Grieving without the possibility of preparing for the departing. This situation includes unconsciousness or a medically induced coma prior to death. The taboo surrounding death, and the cultural unacceptability of talking about it, leads to families not talking about death and related matters. In some cases, they become unable to talk because the patient is unconscious or is taking medication that limits the ability to communicate. This fact must also be taken into consideration when defining the homiletical situation. People who were not present with the dying person because of cultural barriers, like death being taboo, or because of health reasons, like a medically induced coma, and could not openly and effectively communicate about the approaching situation enter the post-mortem period at a disadvantage.

(c) **How the grieving person generally copes with anxiety and stress**. These issues are frequently inaccessible for the minister, but they are relevant and influence the state of the grieving person.

(d) **The existence of previous experiences with grief**. For this parameter, the considerations are positive experiences: "I have already gone through this before, and that gives me hope that I will be able to cope with my loss"; negative experiences: "An unbearable burden and loss from the past weakens me in my current suffering"; and specific cases. An unusual form of previous experience with grieving is the preparation for grieving that can be seen in relatives who take care of patients with long-term, life-threatening illnesses. Their coping process will invariably lead to both positive and negative results. Therefore, it is important that ministers take care of the people in their parish not only after the death is announced, but also in the period when a person is at risk from a serious illness. The case of a family who received pastoral help when they were coming to terms with the diagnosis shows that care during the process of dying is significantly beneficial when they started to grieve. This care resulted in a greater openness in family communication and authentic expressions of fear and pain because preparative grieving had taken place and there had been opportunities to express relationships, love and forgiveness, and to put other matters in order. When a family does not take this opportunity, they enter the grieving process with unnecessary stress factors which could have been dealt with in advance.

(e) **Religious or cultural ties** with accompanying expectations for behaviour or support.

Bereaved and faith in God. Faith in God is an important prerequisite for the funeral sermon to achieve its aims – a prerequisite for spiritually coping with loss and a prerequisite of a readiness to cope with one's own death in a Christian manner. However, I only found one differentiation analysis that referred to the faith of the bereaved.[42] As the normal method of defining the funeral situation does not take into consideration the faith of the bereaved, I am of the opinion that when the homiletical situation is being defined, this criterion is not given enough attention, and sometimes faith is misused as a reason not to grieve, either in the words of the minister or the attitudes of the bereaved.

The words of the minister. At a church funeral, the bereaved can be divided into two groups. One group has some degree of Christian faith in God, and based on it they approach the funeral and the reality it reflects. When speaking to this type of bereaved, ministers frequently express faith in a way which can lead to the grieving process being blocked: "Don't cry; the person is with the Lord." Some of the bereaved stop at the words "Don't cry;" they do not deal with the loss and do not connect to the positive influences of faith which can help them process the loss. Therefore, the minister should demonstrate the eschatological perspective in such a way that it helps the bereaved to cope with their new reality.

A disproportionate approach to loss. In the case of a Christian family with a strong Christian faith, there can be an ability to spiritually accept God's sovereignty even when they experience a personal loss. This attitude was observed in a number of cases, for example the father of twins who tragically lost their lives, or the adult children of an elderly gentleman who was a "patriarch" for many Christians in his vicinity. As they accepted God's sovereignty, the family then concluded that spiritual acceptance of the loss also resulted in coping mentally. But this is a mistake. Therefore, I think that it is important that in this situation the minister endorses the grieving process as acceptable for a Christian without causing doubt about spiritual surrender to God's sovereignty.

The other group of bereaved do not have a positive personal relationship with God or to a particular Christian church.[43] Their motivations for deciding to

---

42. I. Kišš, *Nádej nad hrobom 1*, 35 only in sermon no. 12, "one son religiously indifferent."

43. *Agenda ČCE* (Agenda of the Evangelical Church of Czech Brethren [ECCB], 1983), 194: "In many cases the people who request the services of a minister at a funeral or cremation are very distant from the church or non-Christians who are aware that death is a critical situation that asks profound questions about the true meaning of life. They expect that it is the church that has the right words for this situation. (Form 3)." A similar observation is also made by Carr in *Brief Encounters*, 17. He describes a case where people who don't attend church approach a minister and request the minister to perform religious acts (blessing a cross, home, etc.), and Carr argues that behind this request is often "a simple faith that something is 'there' and it should be recognised."

have a Christian funeral for their deceased are varied, but it does not necessarily mean that they are searching for faith at this turning point in their lives.

It is not right to automatically assume faith in the bereaved. Sheppy makes some insightful comments on this: "Christian funeral rites often assume faith not only in the deceased but also in the bereaved, and this is sometimes implicit in the liturgy and at other times in explicit comments during the funeral rite. But often the minister only finds a faith which was expressed many years ago in baptism, or he does not find any expressions of faith."[44]

(f) The existence of other stress factors in the life of the grieving person. These additional stresses can include financial problems, such as loans which were taken on the basis of the incomes of both spouses. But the bereaved could also have a serious illness, be socially isolated, or be facing other stress factors.

The perception of the events by the bereaved

Authors who take into consideration the pastoral context of funerals[45] claim that many of the bereaved at the funeral are not capable of perceiving reality, and some of those are present "like in a dream."[46] According to Carr, the bereaved only rarely listen to the sermon due to their emotional state.[47] They may be left with isolated observations, but they remember the manner and the attitudes more than the content. Sheppy believes the bereaved only remember "peculiarities and the overall impression which they remember is often a result of a specific characteristic through which they interpret the whole event."[48] If it is true that the bereaved evaluate the whole event through fragmented memories of the rite, then any particular detail can take on a different importance in comparison with someone in a normal state. This implies greater demands on the quality of service and an awareness of the potential importance of every problem, which in a sermon at a standard church service could be graciously overlooked.

In contrast, Palmer takes the opposite view: "For many, when they stand by the grave of a wife or a son with a broken heart, it is perhaps the only time in

---

44. P. Sheppy, *Death Liturgy and Ritual, vol. 1*, 13.

45. W. Carr, *Brief Encounters*, and P. Sheppy, *Death Liturgy and Ritual, vol. 1*.

46. We need to be aware of the defence mechanism of shock, especially in cases of sudden or very painful loss.

47. W. Carr, *Brief Encounters*, 121.

48. P. Sheppy, *Death Liturgy and Ritual, vol. 1*, 15.

their lives when they are reachable with God's truths, and the minister brings on himself an enormous guilt if he misses this opportunity."[49]

In summary, the ability of the bereaved to follow the sermon is dependent on the dynamic of their grief. In the same family, different individuals will feel the loss to a greater or lesser extent. Based on my observations, normally some of those in attendance are able to clearly and rationally perceive everything that is said. If too much emphasis is placed on the observations about the reduced ability to perceive the preaching at the funeral, then it would follow that addressing the bereaved directly at the funeral is ineffective, and it would be necessary to delay it to pastoral contact after the funeral. But such an approach would be unprofitable.

For the sermon itself, these observations can be important in a number of ways:

1. Even in cases when ministers know that the bereaved will not be capable of listening to the sermon, they can address them because our observations show that some of the ideas from the funeral sermon are received by the bereaved after some time has passed through their social ties. If ministers behave in an appropriate way, they equip the relatives and friends to be able to remind the bereaved of the comforting words in the days and weeks after the funeral.

2. Ministers can print out a copy of the sermon and also the whole rite for the bereaved. Some of the bereaved will not be interested in it. Those who accept the funeral sermon and its liturgical setting as a memory of the funeral of their loved one may, during the process of grieving, return to the ideas found there.

3. I believe that the bereaved are usually able to follow and understand the section during which ministers address them directly. At the same time, ministers should only address the bereaved when they want to draw their attention to a certain emphasis in the sermon. In this sense addressing the bereaved is like "knocking" on their doors.

4. Well-prepared pastoral sections of the funeral sermon can also have a missional impact on those in attendance who are not emotionally affected by the death, if ministers convey these sections in such a

49. Ch. Palmer, *Evangelische Homiletik*, 288, cited in Jamnický, *Evanjelické pohrebné kázne*, 33. The completely opposite view is taken by W. Carr, *Brief Encounters,* 121, where he claims "the challenge to accept an unknown structure in that moment is an invitation to reject it."

way that those in attendance recognize an authentic testimony about the importance of faith in the crisis situations of life.

The expectations of the bereaved

The bereaved have diverse expectations in regard to the funeral rite. For the purpose of this study, the bereaved are classified by their view of God and faith: some of the bereaved are searching for what the church has to offer; others want a church funeral but this does not necessarily mean they are searching for Christian motifs.

Requirements which correspond to the pastoral aims of the Christian church. Active Christians for whom being involved in the life of a local church means more than just being part of a social community and has a spiritual dimension, are looking for God and his Word in both the funeral rite and the funeral sermon.

Requirements which do not necessarily correspond to the pastoral aims of the church. Josef Smolík's statement about the revival of interest in occasions for pastoral reasons which, according to him, sociologists found to be "the continuing reach of the community of Lutheran Christians"[50] can still be valid today, but other factors can also play a role. Therefore in connection to the aims of the bereaved in requesting a church funeral, it should not be automatically assumed that this is an expression of their searching for God in a crisis situation in their lives.[51] "Many of them choose a Christian funeral for their relatives because of tradition, other preferences, pressure from within the family or because they do not know that non-religious or humanist funerals are readily available."[52] Carr and Sheppy offer a number of observations from an English perspective. All their observations may not be valid in another cultural context, but nevertheless they serve as a corrective when trying to take into consideration the real expectations someone has when they request a church funeral. The following summary is based on their observations:

The request from certain bereaved for a church funeral does not correspond to the expectations of the church because they have:

1. A different aim: to honour the deceased.[53] Therefore they are not interested in church preaching. From this point of view,

---

50. J. Smolík, *Radost ze slova*, 149.
51. W. Carr, *Brief Encounters*, 29.
52. *Bereavement Care in Practice*, 59.
53. P. Sheppy, *Death Liturgy and Ritual, vol. 1*, 6.

church preaching is merely a "tolerated" part of the rite and not a "desired" part.

2. Other expectations:

   a. A funeral and nothing else. An openness to the church being involved in the rites of passage of these people does not signify an openness to the church directing "all areas of their lives."[54]

   b. The rite but not a sermon. According to Carr, in this case the ritual rather than its content is more important for the people requesting it. Therefore, they critically assess ministers who, according to him, "are preoccupied with the meaning of words" and "expound and and argue over Scripture." From their point of view, "the church and its minister are a resource for expressing of whatever the people wish to express."[55] Carr evidently assumes that in their view, what should be expressed is not kerygmatic content.

3. Other core emphases: There may be a desire for help in dealing with the psychological aspects of loss but no interest in eschatological questions.[56]

4. Other ideas about who conducts the rite. They are burying the deceased, and the priest is only there to conduct the rite. Carr envisages that the people who request the rite to be conducted approach the church as an institution from which they order a service and get what they want. In fact, they "use" the minister to conduct their own rite. On the question of the legitimacy of the participation of the church and the minister in such an event, Carr states that this kind of question cannot be answered by imposing extensive theological prerequisites and expectations on the people who have requested the ritual.[57]

5. Something else is of ultimate importance. Some requests may be for things that are from the church's point of view marginal.

54. W. Carr, *Brief Encounters*, 29.
55. Ibid., 30.
56. P. Sheppy, *Death Liturgy and Ritual, vol. 1*, 104.
57. W. Carr, *Brief Encounters*, see 15 and 30.

If there can be such a variety of attitudes between ministers and those requesting funerals, then Carr may be right when he claims: "Unless the minister can grasp this, then dissatisfaction and confusion will result for all."[58]

The Wider Funeral Congregation

The normal homiletical process requires that ministers, after completing their exegesis of the biblical text, consider the application of their message to the lives of their listeners. At the theoretical level, this approach is generally accepted. Therefore, it is notable that this approach is not generally adhered to at church funerals. The homiletical situation of the funeral is predominantly defined by the case of the deceased, sometimes with reference to the bereaved, but almost always the largest group, the wider funeral congregation, is overlooked. More precisely, they are not overlooked in the wording of the sermon because the minister does address this group, but the theoretical questions about how to convey the biblical message to this group so that they can accept it, identify with it, and, to the greatest extent possible, add it to their values, are not asked.

This critical approach stems from my observations at the crematorium, where I saw that ministers sometimes address the wider funeral congregation only on the basis of what the theology of their church emphasizes, which excludes other Christians, or they are addressed as if they were irreligious, which naturally results in missionary bias. Therefore, ministers should ask the question, "What type of listeners can I expect?" On the basis of the answer, they can uncover the range of issues they need to respond to and then relate them to the message of the biblical text. Not doing this means they cannot enter into an honest dialogue which is a prerequisite for effective delivery of their message. Sometimes though, ministers only find out at the funeral that their assumptions were mistaken.[59]

The congregation at a funeral is generally not like the meeting of a church congregation where those in attendance have common attitudes to life. The opposite is in fact true; the funeral is a diverse gathering where some are indifferent to faith and some even opposed to it. They were connected to the deceased by many different factors, for example, friends with similar interests

---

58. Ibid., 18.

59. Ministers are not the only ones who must come to terms with this problem. In 2009, the television news reported that the Slovak deputy prime minister, at a celebration of the fifth anniversary of the Selye János University in Komárno, read an address aimed at students, none of whom were present.

in an intentionally cultivated relationship, colleagues from work, neighbours in the location where they lived, and members of a local church who shared an expression of religious faith. Often they do not belong to the same social class and have differing attitudes towards religion, Christianity, and to the church that is conducting the rite. Even when all the people involved are from one church community, the participants will not have identical spiritual lives.

Therefore in connection with the faith of those expected to attend the funeral, the questions posed by Judith Wray should be answered:

1. Question: Will the setting be mainly Christian or non-Christian?

2. Question: What is the faith commitment of these people in relation to that of the deceased?

3. Question: What religious beliefs about life and death do they cling to?[60]

These questions are important because a Christian rite assumes both the faith of the deceased and the faith of the bereaved. If these assumptions are not true, those attending may perceive the rite as theatre or even a form of religious aggression.

1. Answer: Ministers may estimate the composition of the funeral congregation, or they can clarify it in conversation with the bereaved when arranging the funeral.

2. Answer: The faith of the deceased may not be identical to the faith of friends and acquaintances. There may be mutual respect but also rejection and even contempt, notwithstanding any admiration of the deceased's professional or human qualities. When ministers take this into consideration, they are able to define the ideas and problems that will be influencing their listeners. If their ministry is to be meaningful for those present, they must be communicative and cannot simply ignore their listeners' thinking, concepts, and use of terms.

    Even when ministers put in maximum effort, they cannot take into account every influencing factor. Therefore, I recommend that ministers restrict their subjective feeling of responsibility to the capabilities they have based on education and experience, and then

60. J. H. Wray, "Preaching Life in the Face of Death," 40.

decide which factors they will respond to. Otherwise they will be unable to even get started with this ministry.

3.   Answer: With regard to religious beliefs, Sheppy maintains that "most of our contemporaries do not see death as the gateway to eternal life."[61] When taking into account the seriousness of this comment, it is not only significant whether the bereaved and the wider funeral congregation know the teachings of the church about death and eternal life, but the crucial question is whether they have made these teachings their own and live by them. Therefore, the circle of people about whom Sheppy's observation is valid may include those who profess to belong to the church. Christian proclamation of the gospel should seek to present the universal claims of Christ in a way that is understandable and does not place unnecessary obstacles to its acceptance by postmodern people.

The following points can be added:

- Responsiveness to the gospel message. The responsiveness of the wider funeral congregation to the gospel is described differently by different authors. The extreme positions can be defined using texts from *Agenda ČCE* (Agenda of the Evangelical Church of Czech Brethren, ECCB) and from Filo's reflections on funeral sermons. *Agenda ČCE* (1983) is based on observations at that time in the Czech Republic and states that the funeral congregation "is not always receptive to the biblical message of resurrection in its confessional form."[62] They are stating that there may be some attending the funeral who reject the message. In contrast to this, Filo's view is that people present are, on the basis of an encounter with death, confronted with questions that mean they are highly receptive to the message: "He listens to see if he will be understood in his uncertainty and in his uncertain searching. He is curious to know whether there are answers to his own hidden fears and if there is a greater certainty that could replace his fickle and often momentary happiness." The wider funeral congregation is simultaneously characterized as "possibly emotionally undamaged, but all those

---

61. P. Sheppy, *Death Liturgy and Ritual, vol. 1*, 103.

62. *Agenda ČCE*, 194.

attending are certainly existentially impacted. At the funeral of another person it is always a bit about me."[63]

I think that Filo is correct in pointing out that the problem of responsiveness to the message is to some extent the issue of how ministers approach the topic. If listeners are going to follow their preaching, it must touch the questions listeners are dealing with and offer a biblical perspective which makes sense to them. What Souček describes as "a proclamation of a new reality which was opened by Jesus Christ with his resurrection"[64] is only possible if listeners are able to perceive the minister's messages as the solution to their situation and not just a decorative thought in a stressful situation. Therefore, I am convinced that ultimately in the current cultural climate, there is a conditional openness to the message, but from the side of the church, this requires taking a whole set of "giant steps" towards the unchurched public.[65] I agree with Bill Hybels about the necessity "to understand the way they think," – how people outside the church think – and also how formal members of the church think. This leads to the need to search for a way of presenting the message that will be understandable to them.

For situational homiletics, this observation means there is a need to philosophically evaluate the existing approaches to verbalization, from the way theological concepts are presented to the attempts, or absence thereof, to meet the thinking of modern people.

- (Un)preparedness to meet with death. Modern people encounter death differently in comparison with people in the past. They are less prepared to bear the consequences that result from the death of a loved one. In the mass media, they may encounter death every day, but being close to death has not been a personal experience. Therefore, they lack the prerequisites required for parting with a loved one as well as for incorporating their own mortality into their framework of existence. This reality is a serious burden on the funeral, but it is a task ministers cannot avoid, which is why I agree

---

63. J. Filo, *Evanjeliové možnosti*, 277. Similarly J. Kubíkova expects that there will be more listeners than usual and that "their hearts will be more open and accessible than at other times – they will be like this particularly at transitional moments in life." *Kažte evangelium*, 166.

64. J. Smolík, *Radost ze slova*, 150.

65. See B. Hybels, "Speaking to the Secularized Mind," in B. Hybels, S. Briscoe and H. Robinson, *Mastering Contemporary Preaching* (Portland: Multnomah, 1989), 29.

with Jürgen Moltmann who states, "What wisdom about life do we gain when we remember that we must die, and what foolishness when we forget that we are mortal?"[66]

- Varied intensities of grieving. There are cases when the death of the deceased affects people who belong to the wider funeral congregation including identification due to age, similar illness, or a good relationship with the deceased, etc. In certain cases, this affect may be complicated by factors that increase the emotional involvement, such as funerals for the victims of violence or tragedy[67] or attending a funeral of an acquaintance not long after the funeral of a loved one.[68] There are times when the whole funeral congregation is in shock, and those who attend must deal with the stressful experience after the funeral.

  But there are also funerals where those attending are uninvolved relationally and are not affected by the grieving. Ministers need to take this into account in their preparation and consider when they will comfort the whole of the funeral congregation and when their comfort will be restricted to the grieving family.

- The loss of a mutual interpretative basis. The situation of contemporary listeners is illustrated by Long when he refers to the relationship between the loss of narrative and the ability to perceive the meaning of events. He declares that from the point of view of ritual, attendance at a funeral represents playing a social role in an extensive civil and religious drama in which we corporately express who we are and what we believe at the time of death. He also states that "from our memories we have lost the central myths and sacred public narrative which would support the greater meaning of events such as attending a funeral." According to him, the decrease in attendance at funerals is related to this because the aforementioned

---

66. J. Moltmann, *In the End – the Beginning*, 119, full quote: "All human life draws towards death. This fact is unalterable. It is the fact that we must die, which distinguishes us from the immortal gods; the fact that we know it which distinguishes us from animals. What wisdom about life do we gain when we remember that we must die, and what foolishness when we forget that we are mortal?"

67. P. Sheppy, *Death Liturgy and Ritual, vol. 1*, 107: At funerals of the victims of violence or tragedy, there is a "public dimension." In this kind of case, according to Sheppy, the principal issue is cosmic theodicy, and he notes that "as Christians we cannot offer a theology of vengeance, but we offer the universal results of the crisis."

68. W. Carr, *Brief Encounters*, 118.

roles in the social rite lose their interpretational basis and personal motives, expressing condolences, for many people are not connected with attendance at the funeral. After reflecting on the crisis of meaning, Long concludes: "We lack a common story about death – secular or religious – and any ritual that lacks a supporting narrative cannot survive in thin air."[69]

The Church Year

In certain cases, it is almost unthinkable not to refer to the meaning of the holy days in the church year. This happens when the funeral is conducted in close proximity to one of these holy days or at sacred times such as Advent, Christmas, or Easter.

The Ministers

The personality of ministers, their ability to empathize, as well as their spiritual and theological suppositions, and even the social position of the church they represent, also determine the homiletical situation because everything ministers do at the funeral can create or damage the conditions for fulfilling its purpose.

Smolík refers to ministers' responsibility by saying, "We are performing in the situation of death in which a person is at a loss for words."[70] This description is important not only from a theological point of view, but also for what ministers experience in the context of the funeral rite. It demonstrates the very serious fact that a funeral sermon is delicately balanced. It can tip to the side of being merely empty words or to the side of being a meaningful message. Unlike a eulogy, in which the focal point is the deceased, ministers can only bring meaningful content when they bring God's Word to the situation of loss. Without this, the funeral sermon will become merely a religious talk which lacks that which is the most essential. Ministers must though bring God's Word as a testimony – as a message that is meaningful for them and has meaning for the funeral congregation.

Ministers are mentioned in connection with the homiletical situation because at the funeral they are in a very prominent position, and in this position,

---

69. T. G. Long, "The Funeral: Changing Patterns and Teachable Moments," *Journal for Preachers* (Easter 1996): 6.

70. J. Smolík, *Radost ze slova*, 150.

they must deal with stimuli from the situation and with their interpersonal contacts. They must be aware that they will have to deal with a number of difficulties as follows:

The burden of feeling responsible. If ministers overestimate the significance of the verbal element of the funeral rite, they may feel overwhelmed by the demands on the intellectual dimension of their work. This is a greater risk for Protestant ministers, and I am aware that if this study is misunderstood, it may even increase that risk. Ministers may be liberated from this pressure in two ways: spiritually – being aware that in the whole process, they are "only" God's instrument;[71] and contextually – being aware that the occasion is part of its context and they contribute to it through their presence.[72] Therefore, it is clear that ministers' responsibility is limited to fulfilling their role and expecting God to act in a way that is not limited to the rational impact of their words.

Ministers being drawn into the grieving community. During the initial phase of observations at the crematorium in Banská Bystrica, I could not understand how the same person could conduct three or four funerals in a row on the same day. I was working on the basis of my experience of the feeling of fatigue I had after most of the funerals I have conducted. A doubling or trebling of this fatigue seemed to me unbearable.

I obtained a certain degree of clarification after speaking to the civil funeral celebrant, Mr Halaj. He informed me how hard it is for him to conduct the funerals of people he personally knew, and in those cases, he deals with grief despite having conducted over 1,300 funerals. Then I arrived at the (untested) hypothesis that the level of stress for ministers correlates to the extent and the dynamic of the relationship with the people in question. The closer their relationship with the deceased or the bereaved, the greater they are drawn into the process of grieving and must allow for a greater degree of stress.

Ministers of a small community will know personally almost all the believers who take part in the life of the church and their family members. Therefore, they often bury their own friends. Since the bereaved often belong to the church, ministers are also drawn into their grieving. Naturally they may try to keep some distance from the proceedings, but their sensitivity to the

---

71. W. Carr, *Brief Encounters*, 31. Ministers can be helped by Carr's statement that "The minister is engaged in a process over which he has far less control than he might think." Naturally this statement should not lead the minister to being less responsible in preparation, but it must lead to seeking faith in the one whose name the minister participates in the funeral.

72. W. Carr, *Handbook of Pastoral Studies*, 151: "The key point to which ministers have to hold is that they are part of that context and by their presence they are contributing to it."

pain of people they like burdens them. This is why many ministers have told me that during their ministry, they have had cases where they struggled with tears during a funeral.

Identifying with the case. In cases where the deceased do not belong to the social group of ministers, but they are able to identify with them for other reasons such as age or family situation, there is also an empathetic sharing of the burden of grieving. Communicating with the family when dependent children are left behind, or if the death caused complicated social or family relationships, are also stress factors.[73]

A specific form of stress can be unresolved feelings of injustice which the deceased caused the minister or feelings of guilt the minister has concerning the deceased.[74]

In order for ministers to be able to understand their own feelings, they need to clarify their personal positon in the proceedings. Wray recommends asking the following questions: "What is my relationship to the deceased? What is my relationship to the mourning community? Am I personally grieving for this person? Does this remind me of other losses? What will be my future relationship to those who hear this funeral sermon?"[75]

For completeness, these questions can be expanded to include: "What am I expecting from my activity at the funeral? Do I believe that the gospel has unique power to help the grieving? Do I know the state of mind they currently have? Do I have legitimate aims or are they my own personal aims?"[76]

The rejection of ministers by the grieving community. Ministers enter into the grieving community, and as socially mature people, they participate in their pain and their coping with it. However, ministers may meet with negative attitudes when they are invited to take the funeral service, but "often he is not

---

73. I visited a seriously ill man who was the only support in their town for his wife. She didn't have any friends. She knew that after his death, she would be completely alone. Before his death, she was already showing signs of mental illness, and after his death, she was admitted to hospital due to mental illness.

74. I was a guest at the annual conference of a local church. One member acted very unreasonably towards the local minister, to which the minister responded with calm. When I asked the minister later why he had reacted in this way, he told me that the person in question had only been redirecting his anger due to his wife suffering from cancer onto a substitute. If the minister hadn't understood the situation of this man, he could have been insulted or felt a sense of injustice.

75. J. Wray, "Preaching Life in the Face of Death," 40.

76. Illegitimate personal aims could be, for example, an attempt to demonstrate that I am professionally proficient or in the case of badly constructed aims, a non-ecumenical approach or theologically unbalanced attempts to gain Christians from other denominations or parishes to my own church or parish.

known or in any personal sense wanted."[77] This approach is very stressful for ministers, and if they do not process it, they could face several risks: allowing funerals to become routine without any broader personal reflection; an internal rejection of ministering at funerals;[78] or damage to their self-image if they do not realize that the observed negative reaction of the bereaved is not connected to their value or the quality of their work. These risks can be observed simultaneously in some cases.

Dealing with strong feelings. The death causes strong feelings in ministers which they cannot express to the grieving or with the grieving, and there is a risk that these feelings may be directed against funeral ministry or against themselves. The latter case, according to Carr, can be a result of "introverted anger may produce apathy, which then diverts energy from a vital piece of public ministry."[79] Therefore, Carr recommends that ministers pay attention to the way they deal with their powerful human emotions.

---

77. W. Carr, *Brief Encounters*, 110.

78. According to Carr, it may result in ministers having a negative attitude to "occasions," and they can regard them as almost unbearable due to the tension between their pastoral assumptions and the theological ignorance of the bereaved. Ibid., 4.

79. Ibid., 115.

3

The Purpose of Funeral Sermons

In this section I will formulate the purpose of funeral sermons as it emerges from the different contexts of how they are understood – as part of a church service, as part of the purpose of a funeral; and as proclamation in a specific homiletical situation.

Purpose of Funeral Sermons as a Part of a Church Service

A funeral rite is a church service.[1] Filo states, "In the first place it is necessary to perceive the funeral as a ministry of God's church. God, in this extreme situation, ministers to the church his holy grace. In this sense it is a service of God."[2] In the context of a secular society, we must remember that understanding a funeral as a church worship service will appear to some in attendance as incomprehensible or bizarre.[3]

Despite these reservations, the fact that a funeral is a church service means that it will have the same aim as a church service: to confess faith in Christ's

---

1. For example, *Agenda ČCE* (Agenda of the Evangelical Church of Czech Brethren [ECCB], 1983), 194 says: "The Reformation placed, at the centre of the funeral devotion, confession of faith in the resurrection." At the same time, however, it also shows that this character could be lost: "Today a funeral in that spirit only occurs where it's the funeral of a professing Christian, a faithful family and Christian church fellowship (Form 1)."

2. J. Filo, *Evanjeliové možnosti*, in J. Filo, *Pohľady do neba*, 276. Similarly Ch. Stebler supports this understanding of the church funeral rite as a church service with the statement that in the German context, they "usually speak of worship (Gottesdienst) or funeral service (Trauerfeier)." *Die drei Dimensionen*, 18. On page 26, he states: "In the Protestant church, the main part of the funeral ritual is celebrated in the form of worship, though often in a compressed and reduced form."

3. P. Sheppy, *Death Liturgy and Ritual, vol. 1*, 103.

victory over death and its implications for the deceased and the bereaved.[4] Therefore, culturally and contextually, comprehensible expressions of the joy of faith should be included. In practice, this can cause two problems: a loss of authenticity when expressions anchored in faith are replaced by religious gestures that the minister does not really believe;[5] and an incomprehensible attitude – even with a genuine expression of the joy of faith, it is impossible to guarantee that it will be comprehensible for the others present.[6]

The church service character of a funeral is also stressed by John Allyn Melloh when he asserts that, "The funeral homily – a word addressed to the congregation in a context of prayer – has as its goal . . . the liturgy itself."[7] Long takes a similar approach. The purpose of a funeral sermon he illustrates using the structure "What not / What yes." In the section "What not," he first states that the funeral sermon is not primarily to support the process of grieving or to celebrate the unique characteristics of the life of the deceased, even though both may be present in a sermon. Then he moves on to the question "What yes," in which he states that a Christian funeral is primarily "to provide a suitable structure and language for the worship of God at the time of death."[8] It is essential to remember this so that the funeral, and the funeral sermon as a part of it, does not lose its basic character and theological legitimacy. At the same time, Aidan Kavanagh contextualizes and clarifies the pastoral dimension

---

4. *Agenda ČCE*, 194: "During the time of the early church, Christians gathered for a funeral in order to confess their faith in the victory of Christ, in which the deceased will have a share at the resurrection. The presence of the resurrected one often manifested itself in celebratory joyfulness." Similar J. Jamnický states: "Therefore, ministers should regard it as the most holy of duties at the grave: to bring people to Christ and this as intimately and directly as possible." *Evanjelické pohrebné kázne*, 47.

5. The listeners are able to judge if ministers are using "hollow phrases" or if they show how faith can help the bereaved to deal with their loss in both the situations of the remaining pain of the loss and the Christian hope as joyful expectations of God's dealing with us.

6. After the funeral at which a minister expressed the Christian hope in the resurrection and spoke about eternal life, one of those attending the funeral told me: "They were most likely happy because they are going to inherit." In this he shifted the source of joy from the preaching to material values.

7. J. A. Melloh, "Homily or Eulogy?," 506.

8. T. G. Long, "The Funeral," 8. Similarly, J. Filo understands the word and prayers during the funeral "as a means of sanctification and thus drawing near to God." *Evanjeliové možnosti*, 276. In this sense, it is possible to view the role of the Christian funeral and the sermon as helping people draw near to God in a crisis moment of life due to the loss of a loved one.

of the funeral sermon and demonstrates that it should not be an event "for" the deceased or the bereaved.[9]

The Purpose of Funeral Sermons as a Part of the Funeral

When attempting to define the purpose of funeral sermons, they should be placed in the context of the funeral as a whole. Therefore, broader questions about the purpose of a funeral must be asked. But funerals are not uniform phenomena. Even though the liturgical structure of the funeral ceremony maintains essential characteristics based on the tradition of each church, the course of the funeral is significantly influenced by:

- Non-religious factors such as the age of the deceased; the manner of the death, for example, by long illness, tragic circumstances, murder, or suicide; and the size of the funeral.[10]
- Religious factors such as the religious life of the deceased and the deceased's position in the church, etc.

These factors must be borne in mind when describing the purpose of a funeral, which can be divided into universal, non-religious aspects, which every funeral fulfils regardless of its religious-philosophical context; and aspects connected to a Christian funeral, in the context of the emphasis of the particular church.

Universal, Non-Religious Aspects of a Funeral

Every funeral, regardless of its religious or non-religious character, has the following aspects: disposal of the deceased's body; a farewell with the deceased; a rite of passage; and coming to terms with human mortality.

---

9. A. Kavanagh, *Made Not Born: New Perspectives on Christian Initiation* (Notre Dame: University of Notre Dame Press, 1976), 126. Quoted in J. A. Melloh, "Homily or Eulogy?," 504: "Neither the [Easter] vigil nor a funeral (nor for that matter a wedding or an ordination) is a liturgy 'for' someone. They are celebrations of the Church, by the Church, and for the Church under the criteria of the gospel." An opposite position is taken by Sheppy: "The funeral is for the dead person, and the mourners meet to say farewell. There is, therefore, the pastoral task of entrusting the mourners to God and of incorporating them into the activity of God in Christ. Yet the Christian minister will surely want to enlarge that purpose. There is the primary ritual task of committing the dead to God, and of entrusting the dead to the Christ who himself died. The dead person is placed at the centre of the rite, and the bereaved gather round." *Death Liturgy and Ritual, vol. 1*, fn. 59.

10. An example of a joint funeral is that following the tragic event on 19 January 2006, when an air accident in Hungary killed forty-two professional soldiers of the Slovak army.

The funeral as the disposal of the deceased's body

The funeral is a hygienic, dignified, and socially acceptable treatment of the deceased's body in such a way that maintains its dignity in that cultural and religious context.[11] In inland Christian Europe, the hygienic disposal of the body is normally interment – the meaning is well captured by the German term *Be-erdigung* – or cremation. A review of funeral rites around the world reveals considerably more ways of disposing the deceased's body, which in different cultures are regarded as acceptable.[12] There is not universal agreement because what one culture regards as a dignified disposal of the body may seem to another culture questionable or problematic. For example, burial at sea, a historical seafaring custom, would for those now living on land exclude the possibility of visiting the grave. The cultural context also contributes to the expressions of mourning. For example, in Russia and Moldova, the custom for the funeral procession is to carry the coffin of the deceased on the back of a lorry, and it is covered with colourful carpets. From the perspective of Slovak culture, that practice does not give the impression of reverence and mourning.

The funeral as a farewell to the deceased

The funeral is generally understood as a farewell to the deceased person. Therefore, the disposal of the body is not the only purpose of the funeral. A life has ended, and has departed from family, work, and social relationships. Those who loved and respected him or her come in order to say goodbye. The death is the primary and main reason for the funeral. Therefore, I regard a farewell to the deceased as one of the main universal roles of a funeral. If this is true, then not mentioning the deceased in the funeral sermon would weaken or make it impossible for this purpose to be fulfilled.

The funeral as a rite of passage

The farewell to the deceased is directly related to the social impact it has on the bereaved. From a sociological perspective, it is a rite of passage,[13] one of

---

11. In history, it has been possible to see the opposite of this – deliberate abuse of the body of the executed, for example, during the Caraffa's slaughter in Prešov (Slovakia) 1687.

12. For example, not only a discrete cremation without the attendance of the bereaved, but also the public cremation of the body in the presence of the funeral congregation. See the Hindu customs in India.

13. For more information, see Arnold van Gennep, *The Rites of Passage* (London: Routledge, 2004).

the ceremonies which accompany the life of a person.[14] After the death of a husband, a wife becomes a widow. Furthermore, this loss sometimes alters her social status and other connected facts.[15]

The funeral as a rite of passage should help the bereaved to accept their new role in life. To become aware of the new reality, they need to see the deceased, the closed coffin, and its interment in the grave. These painful pictures will, for a long time, compete with the subconscious expectation that the deceased will come home, or in some cases with the feeling that even after the funeral, the bereaved spotted the deceased somewhere in a crowd. But they now have available to them an experiential basis for entering into their altered reality.[16] The rite of passage, of course, does not only concern the person at its centre but is of importance for the wider social context.

The funeral as a way of coming to terms with human mortality

Every funeral reminds the funeral congregation of a person's death and is a reminder of the fleeting nature of their own lives. Therefore, coming to terms with mortality occurs at two levels: coming to terms with the loss of a relative or friend and coming to terms with one's own mortality. This reality is communicated to the congregation both non-verbally, for example when, after looking into the coffin of a female student, her peer said, "death has come even to us!" and verbally in the spoken part of the ceremony.

Aspects of a Christian Funeral

If what is said in the previous section is correct, these aspects must also be present at a Christian funeral. It is debatable whether certain roles should be adopted without alteration or whether from the perspective of faith they gain a different emphasis. At the same time, the question "What makes a Christian funeral Christian?" arises. It is possible to identify with Sheppy who

---

14. For example, a wedding is a rite of passage to the state of being married – single people become a married couple. In this, the given individuals, in this case the bride and groom, are accompanied by a section of society. It is similar also with other transitions in life. This role of the funeral is not necessary in cases where the community is saying goodbye to somebody who did not have any close relatives like a life partner or children.

15. The wife of a deceased minister is no longer a minister's wife.

16. It would be beneficial to determine to what extent attending the funeral contributes to a quicker acceptance of the new reality and to an improved handling of the transition.

asks whether a funeral which does not place a theological emphasis on death and resurrection is Christian.[17]

A Christian funeral as the disposal of the body of the deceased

The Christian funeral also has two basic levels: material, disposing of the body of the deceased, and spiritual, liturgical-homiletical. The question is whether the material part remains outside the specifics of a Christian funeral. The liturgical acts, which each church conducts, demonstrate that this part is influenced by their theology.

A Christian funeral as a farewell to the deceased

The Christian funeral is also a farewell because it is completely true that, as Carr excellently expressed and all those bereaved have from time immemorial experienced, "With death the relationship of embodied people is ended."[18] The earthly life of the deceased person has ended, and a period in the life of the bereaved is over. The specific features of the Christian farewell are a testimony on two levels. On the one hand is the pain of farewell because death is a reality for a Christian which radically interrupts relationships. On the other hand, Christians have hope arising from faith in God. A Christian funeral must demonstrate openness to both dimensions of the situation. There is both the pain of farewell and there is faith. Due to faith, we do not have to silence the pain, and due to the pain, we do not need to lose faith.[19]

The pain of loss. In the proclamation of the Word, we need to search for a Christian approach to the loss of the loved one and to the significance of faith in the process of coming to terms with loss. We will only achieve this if we admit that Christians are not immune to the loss of a loved one and that loss is a painful experience. Even when we fully accept the eschatological emphases of the New Testament, we are not exempted from the time-consuming process of grieving. I have observed this in stable, mentally strong Christians who have a rich life of faith and were saying farewell to a loved one who also convincingly practised their faith. Ministers must therefore reassure the bereaved that by grieving they are not denying their faith in God and encourage them to process the loss in a Christian way.

---

17. P. Sheppy, *Death Liturgy and Ritual, vol. 1,* 104.

18. W. Carr, *Brief Encounters,* 114.

19. Cases of faith being lost in life crises are not being dealt with here due to simplification. In our pastoral work, we cannot, of course, allow this. Therefore, it is necessary to pay more attention to the issue of faith in the crises of life both in research as well as pastoral work.

The hope of faith. Belief in the resurrection and eternal life are fundamental to the Christian faith. Therefore, they must not be used in the funeral sermon as painkillers for temporary pain relief. On the contrary, ministers must lead their listeners in such a way that they search for what the biblical message about eternal life and its acceptance in faith means for their current situation, and they must show the bereaved how they can incorporate it into their lives as an indisputable reality without ignoring the pain of loss.

On a critical note, in certain cases there may be an unbalanced approach or even a serious practical theological failure when the words proclaimed – the means of expression as well as the thought concepts – all avoid acceptance of the reality of death. Instead, the resurrection is proclaimed too quickly. This criticism is not trying to question the New Testament emphasis on the resurrection and eternal life, but inappropriate use of this emphasis can cause problems for the bereaved. Christians who take the biblical message about the resurrection and eternal life seriously do not know how they should react to their real loss. They ask the question: Is it a loss or not? The deceased is no longer here (she has died) but she has eternal life before her. "Are we allowed to grieve at all?" Instead of deliberately beginning to grieve, they avoid it and attempt to "be strong." However, they can only be strong after having come to terms with their loss, grief, anger, self-pity, and all other accompanying characteristics of grieving.

On the basis of this, it is possible to state that if a Christian funeral indirectly causes the Christian bereaved to feel that by grieving they are doubting their faith, or even has actively prevented them from grieving, then it is not being biblically truthful or pastorally wise. In such a case, I would have to speak about the theological and practical failing of the homiletical and pastoral work.

A Christian funeral as a rite of passage

A Christian funeral, along with all other funerals, is a social declaration of the new status of the bereaved. A husband has become a widower and a child has become an orphan. Filo highlights that the Christian rite of passage is distinctive as it represents the "deceased and the grieving survivors as members of the church of Christ."[20] Sheppy goes even further, and both the deceased and the bereaved "he entrusts to God's love in Christ."[21] This means that the change of status that occurs due to the death of the deceased takes place in the church

---

20. J. Filo, *Evanjeliové možnosti*, 276.

21. P. Sheppy, *Death Liturgy and Ritual, vol. 1*, 57: "To omit this is not a course we can pursue without failing in our ministry to be a Christian rite in anything other than the words."

context and in relation to God. On the pastoral level, it therefore follows that if the bereaved are members of the church of Christ, then this remains true during the period of loss. Their identity is not only as widowed and orphaned. At the same time as having an altered social status, there is a declaration of the dimension of faith that God cares for widows and orphans. They do not remain alone. They are linked to those who went before us, and they are grafted into a community that endures. The dynamics of the help derived from this truth are dependent on both objective and subjective assumptions: objective, that the bereaved are integrated to the church; and subjective, their perceptions of this truth.

In connection with the ceremony being a rite of passage, Carr notes that "These rites do not exist in a vacuum, they belong to the people involved."[22] From this he concludes that the ceremony takes on the significance that the individual grants it, and he allows for the fact that those who request the rite to be conducted in fact "use" the minister to conduct their own rite. In relation to the questions of whether it is legitimate for the church and the minister to be involved in such an event, Carr states that it is a type of question that cannot be answered by imposing extensive theological prerequisites and expectations on the person who has requested the ritual.

Carr further states that for the bereaved,

> the process of the ritual is more important than the content. Christians are preoccupied with the meaning of words. They expound and argue over Scripture. They are acutely sensitive about the wording of promises, and then become casuistical about the terms used. When, therefore, they are confronted by someone seeking a ritual expression of transition in their life, ministers become agitated about the words used and the promises made. But for the applicant these are rarely the issues. The church and its minister are a resource for the expression of whatever the people wish to express.[23]

My opinion is that we cannot wholeheartedly endorse this argument as it totally undervalues the kerygmatic part of the ceremony. However, I do understand the seriousness of his observation about misunderstandings of the purpose and shifts in the emphasis that ministers must avoid.

---

22. W. Carr, *Brief Encounters*, 30.
23. Ibid., 31.

Sheppy approaches the funeral ceremony and the rite of passage from another angle. When searching for the prerequisites for its significance, he comes to the question of the interpretation of death. The rite of passage of the funeral cannot, according to him, have a Christian meaning "where death has no meaning beyond its finality, where it is a dead end."[24] This means that the faith of the person involved is an important prerequisite for the ceremony to have significance.

If Sheppy is right, and I believe he is, then the church's willingness to oblige those requesting a funeral, as it is described by Carr, could place serious constraints on its meaning. It is therefore necessary to devote increased theological and religious-psychological attention to this whole issue, and it is necessary to search for ways that the funeral sermon can fulfil the role of being the verbal component of the rite of passage in a Christian manner.

A Christian funeral coming to terms with human mortality

The Christian funeral also mediates an encounter with death and the existential necessity to think about one's own death. Therefore, one of the purposes of the funeral sermon should be to help the listeners realize the finite nature of this earthly life and their responsibility towards God for it.

The Funeral Sermon as a Proclamation of the Word in a Specific Homiletical Situation

Right at the beginning of this section, I must quote C. H. Spurgeon: "The grand object of the Christian ministry is the glory of God. Whether souls are converted or not, if Jesus Christ be faithfully preached, the minister has not laboured in vain."[25] Rummage states that funeral preaching should

---

24. P. Sheppy, *Death Liturgy and Ritual, vol 1*, 59: Where death has no meaning beyond its finality, where it is a dead end, there can be no Christian rite of passage for the deceased. The journey for the deceased needs to place the dead in the world of the dead, but in Christian theology the world of the dead is not a world of non-being. The Words of Jesus . . . (Matt 22:31–32) challenge those who consign the dead to non-existence. This call reminds us that the rite of passage takes the dead person into a new world. There is a real passage into another mode of existence, and that existence is one of life.

25. C. H. Spurgeon, *Lectures to My Students* (London: Passmore & Alabaster, Paternoster Buildings, 1877), 179.

communicate a timely message from God's Word.[26] In the following text, I will attempt to unpack in more detail what that means.

The most fundamental way that a Christian funeral differs from a civil ceremony is the awareness that the loss is being experienced before God. This fact should have actually been presented first because it is not only one of the distinguishing features, but also one of the most fundamental aspects of the funeral service, and in this way it influences all the other aspects of the funeral sermon. During a funeral service, it should not be just the deceased, the bereaved, and the wider funeral congregation who are referred to. The message of all the verbal and non-verbal communication should be that God is invisibly present here, and through his Word, he speaks to the situation. He has the ultimate say in the lives of all of us.

The preaching of the sermon, as well as the whole course of the funeral, must point to God so that the believers present leave with the knowledge that the best comfort for the grieving comes from God, before whom one day each of us will appear (2 Cor 5:10).

Non-Christians and formal Christians should have the opportunity to say farewell to the deceased and in an unforced way encounter the gospel, which allows them to think about their own relationship to God through Christ. The word "unforced" here does not mean an unclear presentation. The gospel is an unambiguous call to make a decision. But this decision process cannot take place under pressure from the speaker.

Wray also recommends considering the purpose of the funeral sermon in connection with each specific funeral, which demonstrates the relationship between the homiletical situation and specifically set purpose.[27] Stebler adapts Grözinger's thesis about the aims of pastoral work in the funeral sermon, according to which its purpose is "to achieve the constant permeation of the

---

26. S. N. Rummage, "Redemptive Sermons," 650: "While there is a time and place for the aforementioned types of speeches, our sermon should aim for a deeper purpose: to communicate a timely message from God's Word." J. Foltynovský, *Duchovní řečnictví* (self-published, 1927), 159, saw the aims of funeral sermons as being: (1) revive faith in the immortality of the soul; (2) encourage hope in a happy reunion?; (3) show the route to a joyful and calm death; (4) admonish to a continual readiness; (5) strengthen trust in God's graciousness.

27. J. H. Wray, "Preaching Life in the Face of Death," 40. She suggests asking the following questions: "Is the purpose of this funeral to mourn the loss of someone? To remember/celebrate the life of someone? To anticipate/celebrate the resurrection? To comfort those who mourn? To help people get on with life without the deceased? To encourage others' participation in the values of the deceased? To 'preach the gospel'? What is 'gospel' in this situation?"

horizon of God's history and the story of the individual's life."[28] Sheppy has a similar understanding in his approach to the funeral ceremony of entrusting the grieving to God, "incorporating them into the activity of God in Christ."[29] With some reservations, which will be left out of the discussion, what we can see here is a summary of the purpose of funeral sermons. On the basis of the person's state before God, we are able to see the more detailed purpose of the funeral sermon.[30] For people who are "in Christ," Christians who are practitioners of their faith, there are pastoral aims.[31] For secular people who do not have or have lost their relationship to God, there are the evangelistic aims of the funeral sermon (see ch. 3).

The Pastoral Purpose of the Funeral Sermon

In this section, attention will be paid to the context to the pastoral dimension of funeral sermons, the pastoral purpose of the funeral sermon, and supporting observations.

The context to the pastoral dimension of funeral sermons

When ministers sensitively handle the case, pay attention to the bereaved, and conduct the funeral in a dignified Christian way, their work does not just have a homiletical and liturgical dimension, but also a pastoral one. But the pastoral dimension of the funeral sermon must be by definition a part of comprehensive pastoral care of the grievers.[32] It cannot be limited to what is said during the

---

28. A. Grözinger, "Seelsorge als Rekonstruktion von Lebensgeschichte," in *Wege zum Menschen* 38 (Göttingen: Vandenhoeck & Ruprecht, 1986), 185, quoted in Ch. Stebler, *Die drei Dimensionen*, 54. Grözinger continues: ". . . that an integration of the history of God with men and the individual life story succeeds."

29. P. Sheppy, *Death Liturgy and Ritual, vol. 1*, 60.

30. Also, *Agenda Církve československé husitské* (Praha: Blahoslav, 1997), 3, notes the dual nature of the funeral ceremony "pastoral-diaconal and at the same time Kerygmatic-missionary." This supports my definition of the aims.

31. H. H. Jenssen defines the role of the funeral sermon with the expression "seelsorgerliche Verkündigung" (pastoral preaching); from this definition comes an emphasis, and possible suppression, of certain roles. "Die kirchliche Handlungen," in *Handbuch der Praktischen Theologie, vol. 2*, 178.

32. A Roman Catholic funeral has the aim of acting for the benefit of the deceased through intercessory prayers and for the benefit of the bereaved through comfort. A funeral in a Protestant church concentrates on helping the bereaved and not acting for the benefit of the deceased. For the same reasons, Protestants do not practise praying for the dead. See *Agenda ČCE*, 195: "Prayers for the dead as we encounter in the Roman Catholic tradition, the reformers rejected because of concerns that they would be regarded as good works that attempted to earn the salvation of the deceased. It only knows prayers 'Communion of saints' (*communio*

funeral sermon. It is evident that a few personalized sentences during the funeral sermon cannot fulfil all the minister's responsibilities. It would be a good witness for the gospel if it became a standard part of pastoral work that those grieving would receive care from their church before the funeral, during the ceremony, and after it.

Pastoral care of the bereaved before the funeral

The need for pastoral care before the funeral as an expression of care for the bereaved, and not just a practical requirement for obtaining information about the deceased, is found for example in Jenssen.[33] He is certainly not the only author who takes this view and I agree.[34] A comprehensive description of the purpose of pastoral care before the funeral is not within the scope of this study. Its content does not belong to the discipline of situational homiletics but to pastoral theology or pastoral care. Nevertheless, a few notes were added about this in chapter 2, the homiletical situation of the bereaved, and here some ideas which Sugden and Wiersbe present as prerequisites for the funeral sermon to have an effective pastoral dimension:

1. A solemn attitude towards death and dying. They appeal directly to ministers that it should be "a law of the Medes and Persians" that nobody will ever make jokes about death or tell funeral jokes in public gatherings in their churches. They justify their challenge by saying that they have seen some people "crushed when a guest speaker tried to liven up a service by telling a joke about a funeral. People with broken hearts come to the church for comfort and encouragement and not to have their hearts broken again."[35]

2. All pastoral work of ministers has significance as preparation for a situation of loss. Sugden and Wiersbe appeal to the minister to preach "as a dying man to a dying people, and when death does

---

sanctorum) after the Lord's supper in which thanks is given for the testimony of the deceased. We do not address the deceased or mention them by name."

33. H. H. Jenssen, "Die Kirchliche Handlungen," in *Handbuch der Praktischen Theologie*, vol. 2, 189: "A pastoral conversation with the bereaved is a prerequisite for all funeral preaching."

34. H. F. Sugden and W. W. Wiersbe, *Confident Pastoral Leadership: Practical Solutions to Perplexing Problems* (Chicago: Moody, 1973), 103: "As soon as you hear of a death in a church family, try to contact the family. Perhaps you should phone first and see if a visit is in order. It is usually best to get to the home as soon as possible, no matter what hour of the day or night. We may set hours for counselling people but not for comforting people."

35. Ibid.

come, both you and your people will be prepared."[36] While the whole of life is preparation for our departure, these comments will only have an impact on active Christians who are attending the funeral service.

3. Pastoral support. Within the pastoral context of the funeral rite, Sugden and Wiersbe appeal to ministers to accompany the bereaved, and by this support them, when they go for the first time to view the deceased in the chapel of rest. For the bereaved it is a critical time, and the presence of the minister helps the whole family. Therefore, they advise ministers to enter with the bereaved to the chapel of rest and there to stand in silence. Because their presence becomes a sermon, it is not necessary to preach with words.[37] These requirements may seem to be more than the usual ones, but from my own experience, I know that visiting a dying relative and later viewing the body is a very stressful experience. Therefore, whenever ministers are able to provide this support, they should.

4. Social reactivity. Sugden and Wiersbe appeal to the ministers that during their visits to the bereaved, they should carry out their ministry quietly. Verbose or loud pastors can do more harm than good. They should listen and express a willingness to help. The visit should not be long, and any readings from the Bible or prayers should not be routine as they could increase the pain.[38]

5. Thankfulness for the life of the deceased. According to Jenssen, a part of the pastoral conversation before the funeral should be helping "to give thanks for the life of the deceased."[39] He sees a problem in the conflict between the bereaved's recent experience of a painful farewell or even a negative evaluation of the fate of the deceased and our role to encourage thankfulness that reflects the whole life of the deceased. I believe that this role has a pastorally legitimate place in the funeral sermon.

---

36. Ibid., 104.
37. Ibid.
38. Ibid., 103.
39. H. H. Jenssen, *Die kirchliche Handlungen*, 189.

The pastoral dimension of the funeral sermon

The funeral sermon itself must have a clearly developed pastoral dimension. The proclamation of the gospel needs to provide targeted help for the listeners who are grieving. But if the sermon is to be effectively developed, it is essential that ministers know the specific situation of the bereaved, which often turns out to be a sticking point. It is precisely the lack of pastoral care before the funeral, or its reduction to the bare minimum of just collecting basic information about the deceased, that leads to effective pastoral participation in the funeral not being achieved for people who have a weak relationship to the church and the minister.

Earlier in the comments about the homiletical situation of the funeral, it was stated that the funeral sermon is heard in a specific situation of loss. Each individual the sermon is addressed to has different assumptions and needs that should be taken into consideration in the sermon. Therefore, it is essential that more attention is devoted to the characteristics of the homiletical situation of the funeral. But instead of this, I regularly encounter the fact that ministers from different church traditions, if they did not personally know the family of the deceased, did not have sufficiently detailed information about the homiletical situation at their disposal while preparing the funeral. That means they lacked information about the pastoral needs and assumptions of the mourning family.

This lack is reflected in the choice of text, which is not chosen in a way that allows the emphasis of the text to be pastorally developed to the individual needs of those grieving, while at the same time taking into account how their basis of faith influences their processing of the situation. Due to underestimating the need to study the homiletical situation, not only is the directness of the preaching reduced, but also ministers risk their work losing any significance for those grieving.

Ministers who address the bereaved during the funeral sermon must have in mind everything of a personal nature they can, and in fact must also tell them after the funeral during the long period of special pastoral care. As part of the funeral sermon, ministers can only allude to issues in a way that is socially acceptable.

Pastoral care after the funeral

For this period of care also, ministers can find significant help in the academic literature about the psychology of grieving, or "grief counselling." The previously quoted Sugden and Wiersbe recommend that ministers visit the bereaved as soon as possible after the funeral and that they should look out for any signs of emotional problems. They should make the bereaved aware that during these difficult days, they are at the bereaved's disposal. Ministers should also notice any signs of tension in the family as the grieving process has a tendency to open old wounds and arouse feelings of guilt in people.[40]

Pastoral purpose of the funeral sermon

The pastoral purpose of the sermon can be based on observations about coming to terms with loss or an analysis of the suggested purposes which are found in the academic literature and its classification. As the results from these two methods to some extent overlap, they are presented here as a summary. It is not an attempt to "get them back to normal." Sheppy, on several pages of his work, is highly critical of how certain counsellors understand their ministry to the grieving – as supporting them to "get back to normal."[41] In support of his critical approach, he uses both psychological as well as theological language.

As part of his psychological approach to the problem, he states that attempts to get them back to normal may reveal regressive characteristics, which would not be healthy.[42] He references van Gennep to demonstrate that "an attempt to return back to normal means a failure to achieve an incorporation of the new, because 'returning back' is significantly different to 'going through.'"

As a part of theological language, Sheppy says that instead of an attempt to re-establish the old normality, there should be an appeal to "discover the resurrection now and a transformed way of life."[43] From this I understand that working towards the acceptance of altered factors, and their impact, belongs to a healthy spiritual life as well as a step-by-step searching for what it means to follow Christ in this new situation.

Comforting the grieving

Ján Jaminický questions whether an attempt to comfort should be a part of a funeral sermon. He is aware of the opinion of Nierbergall who thinks that it should not be part of the funeral sermon but should be done in a private

---

40. H. F. Sugden and W. W. Wiersbe, *Confident Pastoral Leadership*, 104.

41. P. Sheppy, *Death Liturgy and Ritual, vol. 1*, 11: "I am eager to resist the widely accepted notion that the aim of ministry to the bereaved is to 'get them back to normal.'" He returns to his criticism of this approach on 49 and 83.

42. Ibid., 83.

43. Ibid., 49.

pastoral visit.[44] Despite this, Jaminický argues that comforting has a rightful part in the funeral sermon,[45] and I also hold a similar opinion. After all, a funeral is understood as public grieving, so it follows that public comforting should be included in the same context. Naturally, the theological arguments go much deeper, and after examining Jesus in the Gospels, there is no doubt that comforting the grieving is a legitimate role of the funeral sermon. This position is expressed in documents about funeral rites and sermons of different Christian churches and is also reflected in situational-homiletical aids.[46]

Therefore, it is surprising that in practice it is possible to encounter cases where ministers express the purpose of the funeral sermons with the words: "to preach the Word and not to support the processing of grief." According to my hypothesis, this approach is due to an unbalanced reaction to cases where the message is lost because the funeral sermon is constructed on eulogizing or psychology. At the same time, I completely agree with the opinion that ministers should not, due to supporting the processing of grief, abandon the proclamation of the Word, and they should not redirect their work to content that does not relate to Scripture and proclamation. But they must search for how the message can relate to the situation of their listeners.

Efforts to protect the preaching-approach are theologically legitimate and the duty of ministers. On the other hand, we consider the negation of comforting as incomprehensible because where the Word of God is preached, such an alternative does not exist. Comforting the grieving is an important Christian task. All Christian preaching at funerals is based on the belief that nothing can comfort the Christian like God's Word which brings

---

44. F. Niebergall, *Die Kasualrede* (Göttingen: Vandenhoeck & Ruprecht, 1905), 163, in J. Jamnický, *Evanjelické pohrebné kázne*, 75, argues that "comforting is such a tender spiritual-shepherding task that it should not be carried out *coram publico* but comforting belongs either to a pastoral visit, which the priest should conduct immediately after the death of a member of the church and especially a few weeks later, or in the dignified surroundings of an intimate room in the crematorium immediately preceding the burial. By the grave it should be more common to express general comforting thoughts about how a Christian should behave in difficult times" (163). On 171, he again speaks as follows: ". . . more intimate tones . . ., and various comforting thoughts belong to more intimate circles, specifically at home."

45. Ibid., 77: "I think that the more people appear and prove to be heartless, the more we need to publicly demonstrate compassion and comforting Christian love. This also applies to Christian nurturing and to educating people about Christian *koinonia*. . . . Heartlessness and indifference of people is not yet a reason to leave out from funeral sermons a moment of publicly comforting those grieving."

46. For example, B. Chapell says, "Remember your primary task is to comfort, not to evangelize. Even though evangelistic truths are presented, this is a funeral sermon. The main purpose is to bring the hope of the gospel to loved ones facing the pain of death." *Christ-Centered Preaching: Redeeming the Expository Sermon* (Grand Rapids: Baker, 2000), 346.

encouragement, exhortation, and comfort wherever it is needed. On the basis of this, I regard it as an unnecessary loss for the proceedings if ministers, in an effort to offer comfort, do not take advantage of the tools that are offered by the biblical message, and in place of this they reach for alternative tools. Therefore, the loss of the Word from the funeral sermon must be avoided, since it would cease to be a sermon, as well as unbalanced reactions to psychological approaches because new problems could be created.

The conclusion based on the above is that ministers should preach in such a way that those listening to the sermon are helped to a Christian understanding of their lives and that the bereaved are able to perceive the pain of loss in the light of the hope of faith.[47] The funeral sermon must become a source of effective comfort. Actual observations prove that this is possible. A number of believers stated that, in the situation which they regarded as the hardest in their lives – when they stood by the coffin of a loved one – they could experience both great pain but also be aware that God is with them.

Sources of comfort

Comfort through the presentation of the biblical message. Bryan Chapell gives the challenge "comfort and reach with gospel hope."[48] Jaminický expresses it with more detail when he sees the source of comfort in the certainty "of the Christian faith that believers in Christ have been gifted redemption from the power of sin, eternal death, and condemnation, and it's up to them if they truly achieve it."[49] In the study by Filo, it is observed that this comfort must have both a christological[50] and ecclesiological dimension.[51]

Comfort without a biblical starting point. Practical observations reveal that ministers sometimes present the biblical message without a relationship to those grieving. The possibility to use this relationship to comfort them is lost, and ministers attempt to comfort the grieving by expressing their compassion.

---

47. It is different when Christians bid farewell to a person who was religiously indifferent or an atheist. Bereaved believers when saying farewell find help in God for processing their grief, but at the same time the absence of faith in the deceased is a burden for them.

48. B. Chapell, *Christ-Centered Preaching*, 344. In this he places side by side two roles, pastoral and missionary, and at the same time also the spiritual and pastoral-psychological emphases of the pastoral aims of funeral sermons.

49. J. Jamnický, *Evanjelické pohrebné kázne*, 60.

50. J. Filo, *Evanjeliové možnosti*, 279: "The intensity and value of every other comfort recedes before the comfort that is salvation in God's son Jesus Christ."

51. Ibid. "He simultaneously presents the deceased and bereaved as members of Christ's church."

This kind of approach is seen in ministers who have a high level of empathy, and when they are preparing the funeral sermon, they pay inadequate attention to biblical-theological work. An emphasis on the social dimension, while suppressing the preaching dimension, means they are changing the tools they are equipped with. Their work loses what is specific about a church funeral – the Word – and even though it has certain church characteristics, in terms of tools, it is shifting to the area of a civil funeral. Unlike a civil funeral which clearly states its position, this creates an obscure conceptual approach which is focused on offering a short-term experience of social support instead of fellowship while listening to God's Word. Those attending the ceremony may evaluate this approach positively, but, after everybody else leaves, the "loved ones" remain alone to grieve without the support of a transcendent reality. Therefore, greater attention needs to be paid to this risk both in theoretical work and as a part of field research.

Theologically inappropriate attempts at comforting the bereaved

Jaminický attempts to name some negative attempts at comforting the bereaved that can be found in sermons which are (1) pseudo-Christian negativism towards this earthly life; (2) rationalizing the loss in cases of premature death of a child; and (3) comforting without the necessary prerequisites in the bereaved.

1. Pseudo-Christian negativism towards this earthly life.[52] This approach calls into question ministers' excitement about "the worldview of the Bible," and also it is "an indirect denial of the internal power of Christianity that enables a person to rise above various bitter relationships of our earthly lives." In my opinion, such an approach may be more of a reflection of the fatigue of ministers to their current situation rather than their theological attitude to the world.

2. Rationalizing the loss in cases of premature death of a child.[53] This involves "referring to the fact that by an early death they escaped from the temptation of sin, all kinds of adversities, dangers and suffering of the earthly life and pointing out the fact that how much worse any other manner of death would have been." Such an

---

52. J. Jamnický, *Evanjelické pohrebné kázne*, 65: "When ministers comfort those mourning with the message that the people who are happy are those who through a timely death have been freed from the temporary burdens which caused them to suffer."

53. Ibid., 63.

approach must be evaluated as theologically and philosophically immature.[54]

3. Comforting without the necessary prerequisites in the bereaved.[55] The previous comments from Jamnický were accepted, but in relation to his criticism of the use of theologically legitimate means due to insufficient prerequisites, or their non-existence in the bereaved, the questions arise: What consequences does this have for ministers? Should they retreat from the Christian hope of eternal life? Or should they, in spite of the accuracy of Jamnický's observation, attempt to influence the ideas and presuppositions of the bereaved community and use these comments to comfort the bereaved? This topic requires a separate assessment based on a more in-depth study of the context. It would be a mistake to build on non-existent presuppositions, but to the same extent, it would be a mistake to refrain from proclaiming the hope of faith, because in doing this ministers would abandon the most significant part of their ministry.

The support of faith

It is pastorally important that funeral sermons include a reflection on the philosophical context of the personal experiences of the bereaved. This means that ministers cannot avoid the question of theodicy which is not dealt with in this work.[56]

The same event impacts different people in different ways. This is also true in the case of the loss of an emotionally significant person to death and the impact of this on the faith of the grieving person. During my observations, it was possible to observe that the relationship between faith and the way a person experiences the loss was expressed in two completely contradictory

---

54. Ibid., 64: "The idea that people, through an early death, escape from the temptation to sin that would have surely beset them had they lived longer, is not possible to be considered as Christian. After all Christianity does not command us in this manner to flee from sin and the world but on the contrary to battle against sin and overcome the world."

55. Ibid., 64: "It is very problematic to comfort with peace and blessed peace in heaven; people are unable to understand this reality of the Christian faith, until they are able to, from their soul, sincerely confess that what God does is completely good."

56. During a personal consultation with Prof Kišš, he stated: "In folk religions they typically attribute everything to God. God permitted evil in the beginning, but the book of Job shows that it is the devil who tests humans. There are also natural disasters and instances where bridges or stadiums collapse – God is not guilty but the structural engineer or the builder."

versions – at times as an experience of God's help to cope with the loss and in other cases as a crisis of faith.

Loss and the dynamic experience of God's presence and help. This group of bereaved can be represented by a mother whose thirteen-year-old son died after a short illness. She told me that in the time just after his death, she experienced the worst time of her life – and yet simultaneously, "I had never experienced God's help and closeness – it was as if the Lord Jesus was always with me."

Loss and a crisis of faith. In certain cases, Christians who are bereaved do not find help in their faith. I have come across cases when, after the death of a loved one, they felt desolate and disappointed. They even felt that they had lost God and that he does not exist. Others struggled with the fact that they direct at God the typical anger that accompanies bereavement, and they are afraid to admit it to themselves. Therefore to make the automatic assumption that if a person is a Christian, they will find help in their faith will not always be correct.

This observed difference in how different bereaved people experience their faith I can only describe but not clarify. I am aware of the opinion that those who lose their faith in a crisis did not really possess faith before the crisis. I regard this opinion as problematic because it is not a comprehensive reflection on the problem. It is an oversimplified conclusion that may be true in certain cases. I must give a warning that simplified interpretations can later cause pastoral harm. A minister must bear in mind that Jesus, during his crucifixion, experienced abandonment by God (Matt 27:46), but his fellowship with the Father before this crisis began would not be questioned by anyone. Although I am unable to interpret this phenomenon, ministers must recognize it so that they do not construct pastoral work on unreal premises or not prompt those whose loss has led them to have a negative attitude to God to deepen this attitude.

A number of authors have focused on the problem of faith in the case of the loss of a loved one. However, they have two different perspectives: an evangelistic and a pastoral perspective.

Evangelistic perspective–"to bring forth and deepen faith." According to Metzger, the funeral sermon should

> preach and bring the gospel as a promise . . . to specific people in their particular situation so that faith would be brought forth and deepened . . ., which is hope in temptation, grasping our calling in Christ, . . . and help the person to understand the gospel and thus to salvific knowledge "for the individual," so that they, in the

particular moment of life, could encounter God and could trust in him.[57]

Metzger starts from theological assumptions about effective pastoral work. Faith in response to the message creates the conditions for overcoming a personal crisis due to the loss of an emotionally important person. This approach is theologically, and I believe also psychologically, legitimate as it helps the person in a crisis situation to find a stable point in fellowship with God as the foundation for a new orientation in the altered situation.

Pastoral perspective – "to protect faith." Filo observes that

> the funeral sermon is a necessary aid to faith that is endangered by grief. A confrontation with death is at least a test if not a threat to faith. . . . The faith of one touched by the death of a loved one requires help so that God remains in their consciousness not only as a powerful ruler but also as a loving father. This is the aim of ministry to the bereaved as well as the aim of a funeral sermon.[58]

Ministers therefore must remember that they will address people who are at risk of losing their faith, and they must be very responsible in how they deal with them.

A brief note on the theological aims in the case of severe grief: Jenssen recommends that ministers in cases of severe grief do not directly focus on strengthening trust in God's goodness and love but "encourage acceptance of the lordship of God as it is exemplified in Job 1:21 and 1 Samuel 3:18."[59] It is necessary to critically evaluate this approach, but to me it seems appropriate, especially when ministers have the opportunity to begin more intensive pastoral care with the people involved.

---

57. M. Metzger, *Kasualien* (Evangelisches Kirchenlexikon 3, Vandenhoeck and Ruprecht, 1962), pg 297, quoted in J. Smolík, *Radost ze slova*, 150. Similarly, Mark E. Chapman says, "Funerals are for the living, so that Christ might be called forth in their lives to give them faith and hope and peace, to 'see in death the gates to eternal life' (as the funeral service has it), and so call forth an end to their grieving by the power of the word of Christ." "The Authentic Word in the Face of Death: Reflections on Preaching at Funerals," *Currents in Theology and Mission* 22, no. 1 (Fall 1995): 42.

58. J. Filo, *Evanjeliové možnosti*, 277.

59. H. H. Jenssen, *Die kirchliche Handlungen*, 187. This recommendation is on the basis of the work of Ulrich Neuenschwander (Glaube: Eine Besinnung über Wesen und Begriff des Glaubens, 1957), which comes to the conclusion that the foundational element of faith is not trust in God's love, "but the acceptance of our infinite dependence on God whose creation I am." See also Jenssen, *Die kirchliche Handlungen*, 192: "If we do not begin with the dependence of existence, we avoid the structure of true faith."

Support of grieving and the acceptance of the altered reality

Intrapersonal coping with loss can be observed to consist of a number of levels which people concerned need to deal with: entering into the process of grieving, in which they need to come to terms with the loss of the object; coming to terms with an altered attitude towards oneself, and coming to terms with the impacts on their future. As the grieving process and its possible support or blocking represents a separate issue at church funerals, it will be paid greater attention. The other above-mentioned points I will deal with later.

Supporting the grieving process. Christians perceive the pain of their loss and do not attempt to run from it. They experience their pain in front of God and with his help. Therefore, the funeral sermon should also create a space where those grieving can admit their pain without any questioning of the quality of their Christian life. Thus, it is possible to consider "being freed to grieve"– support to accept the altered reality and personal coming to terms with it – as one of the significant functions of a funeral sermon.

The inclusion of support for coming to terms with loss into the funeral sermon requires theological and pastoral wisdom. Ministers need to understand the impact of the loss and the Christian perspective of how to come to terms with it. Therefore, it is important that what they say reveals that they know that because of death, a living relationship with the deceased has ended, and also the eschatological perspective of faith.

In practice appropriate approaches can be encountered, yet we also encounter the blocking of grieving by both sides: blocking by ministers and blocking by the bereaved.

The risk of ministers blocking the grieving process. Interpretations of the biblical text in the sermon which do not allow for grieving or actively argue against grieving by Christians are theologically unbalanced and cause psychological problems for the bereaved. If we compare the motives that can lead to the blocking of grieving according to Jamincký and those that form the background to the observations by Jenssen, it can be concluded that this collection of motives can come about from theological error and an inadequate expression of empathy, when ministers feels that they must comfort in every way and at any cost.

1.   Blocking grieving due to *theological error.* Jenssen warns against appeals for "excessive heroism due to faith," because this kind of approach more hardens than helps.[60] I wholeheartedly agree with

---

60. H. H. Jenssen, *Die kirchliche Handlungen*, 187.

his statement. Ministers must respect the true state – the need to grieve – and they must not block it.[61] Otherwise their actions will not solve problems but in fact create new ones in at least two ways.[62] In people weakened due to the loss of a loved one, it creates a feeling that there is a deficit in how they express their faith.[63] In cases where the bereaved agrees to such a "game" and they "are strong," it can lead to blocking the processing of the loss[64] and a fossilization in the unprocessed state.[65]

Ministers, instead of doing this, should point in the direction of the place in the battle of faith to which we should get, to the potential to rely on faith, and, if possible, to expressions of the bereaved's faith that they are able to observe during the preparation for the funeral. If ministers notice a significant stabilizing impact of faith as a living testimony about truly coming to terms with loss, they can thank God for it with the bereaved. But they cannot on any account take it for granted or regard it as an automatic expression of every grieving Christian. The homiletical requirements of the funeral sermon must not block the process of processing the loss and grieving because that would be just sweeping the problem under the carpet. On the

---

61. Apart from the problems this approach can cause the grieving, ministers also create doubts about themselves because this approach can be due to theological error, from personal immaturity, or from an inadequate coming to terms with their own mortality.

62. T. Brocher, *Wenn Kinder trauern* (Reinbek: Rowohlt, 1985), 66. C. Hürlimann, *Ich will mit dir gehen. Vom Umgang mit Trauernden* (Zürich: Theologischer Verlag, 1981), 5, states the serious problems which can result from blocking the grieving process of children: "Deferred and prevented grief, which has been encapsulated, can become a kind of time bomb, whose release has unpredictable consequences."

63. The counter productivity of suppressing grieving is demonstrated by Sheppy, *Death Liturgy and Ritual, vol. 1*, 50, with a reference to C. M. Parkes, *Bereavement: Studies of Grief in Adult Life* (London: Penguin, 1986), fn. 158.

64. J. Moltmann, *In the End – the Beginning*, 123: "People who shut themselves off from the mourning process or who cut it short will discover in themselves insurmountable depression and increasing apathy. They will lose contact with the reality of the people around and will be unable to find new courage for living. The person who mourns deeply has loved greatly. The person who cannot mourn has never loved. It is true that at the present time and in our present culture we are so conditioned that we want to have happiness without pain, and love without grief."

65. Ch. Hürlimann, *Ich will mit dir gehen*, 4: "The American funeral director Roy Nichols describes the fate of a woman who, after the death of her husband, took sedatives and immersed herself in incessant activity. She was 'brave.' The result was that after eighteen months, she still maintained her home as a museum to her dead husband; it was even arranged in his favourite colours (Kübler-Roß, *Reif werden zum Tode*, 133). She had not said farewell and she was not free to live a new life."

contrary, the bereaved need to be "freed to grieve," – we must speak about grieving as a phenomenon that exists alongside strong and healthy faith and open an approach to grieving that is conscious and fully accepted by Christians.[66] For those who welcome help, it must open up the possibility of pastoral accompaniment through the period of grieving. The word "must" is being used here consciously and deliberately. Individual pastoral support of those grieving is a duty of the church ministers, although there are few examples of it being conducted in an effective manner in my environment.

2.   Blocking grieving on the basis of an *inadequate expression of empathy*. According to Jamincký, it is a serious mistake that "some ministers regard it as a major responsibility for multiple reasons to drive away all pain and sadness."[67] Against this kind of approach he does not argue psychologically, fleeing from dealing with grief, but theologically, because "God's sending of sadness and pain follows his educational purposes (see Rom 5:3–5), which in our humanity we must not frustrate."[68]

Based on a superficial examination, it seems that Jamincký should be opposed. Yet after a closer look at his approach, it is possible to note that ministers should not miss the opportunity to enable the bereaved to mature. In their pastoral approach, they should work in a way that achieves short-term aims – here we are thinking of short-term comfort – that does not make it impossible to achieve more important long-term aims, which should have significance for the affected person.

The risk of the bereaved blocking the grieving process. Sheppy observed that "for certain Christians, grieving seems to be inappropriate. Death is the gateway to life therefore we should rejoice – even when in pain. Those who want to celebrate in this way say that they are thanking God for the life of the deceased.[69] If the bereaved are capable of giving thanks for the life of the

---

66. J. Moltmann states, "But if this is true we must take, or leave ourselves, just as much time for mourning as for love. It is only the grief which is accepted and suffered-through which restores the love for life after a death." *In the End – the Beginning*, 122.

67. J. Jamnický, *Evanjelické pohrebné kázne*, 59.

68. Ibid.

69. P. Sheppy, *Death Liturgy and Ritual, vol. 1*, 103, and he continues: "Yet even this apparently good response can bring its own problems. If unchecked, it may lead to glossing over death – almost to the point of denying its reality. It is, perhaps, unsurprising that the words

deceased, this is fine. But it is not fine if at the same time they cannot find a place in their Christian thinking for coming to terms with pain.

We know that faith is significant for successfully coming to terms with loss. However, in specific pastoral cases, the question is how people make use of the assumptions of faith to process their loss. If they do not want to accept the loss and wish to remain "strong" and "thankful to God," they themselves block the processing of their loss, and in the course of time we can expect signals that will be their way of searching for help. In these cases, religious expressions lose their value as testimonies of faith and become an escape mechanism or an act of running away from an unbearable truth.

This practice, where faith ceases to face reality and is used as an escape mechanism, I cannot evaluate positively. On the contrary, it must be evaluated as damaging for the person concerned and for the cause of the gospel. By saying this I do not wish to deny the existence of cases where the bereaved may have come to terms with the upcoming loss during a long process of dying. Likewise, I am not disputing the existence of martyrs for whom an expression of their faith was that they were able to accept their own death or that of their loved ones and were able to encourage them. An example of this is found in the history of the Swiss Anabaptists when at the execution of Felix Manz, his mother shouted out words of encouragement.[70] But even here, it should be recognized that the existence of historic testimonies about the behaviour of Christians during the martyrdom of their loved ones is not at the same time a testimony that they did not need to come to terms with their loss.

Accepting the altered reality and processing grief. In the intrapersonal coming to terms with loss, there are a number of levels with which the affected person needs to deal:[71] (1) coming to terms with the loss of something; (2) coming to terms with changed attitudes to yourself; and (3) coming to terms with the questions about the implication of the loss for your future.

1.   Coming to terms with the loss of something. Immediately after the death, the bereaved have a problem in accepting reality. This creates a question about how the minister should communicate with them.

---

of Scott-Holland 'Death is nothing at all' are so popular."

70.   See W. R. Estep, *Příběh křtěncú. Radikálové Evropské reformace* (Praha: Bratrská jednota baptistů, 1991), 40.

71.   I defined these "levels of coming to terms with loss" in 2008. The first impulse came from observing the behaviour of a pensioner who had lost her purse containing a large amount of money. Later I came to the conclusion that these post-loss reactions exist also after non-material loss, which includes the loss of a loved one.

To this question there are contradictory answers: (a) it is necessary to support the acceptance of reality, or (b) it is necessary to avoid referring to the loss as the bereaved's perceptions are overloaded.

a.   A necessity to support the acceptance of reality. In Belfast, I met with a minister who was at the same time a medical doctor with his own surgery. Over the course of a number of conversations, he explained to me that for a terminally ill patient, it is essential to have a seamless transfer from medical care being dominant to pastoral care being dominant, without neglecting what is still medically possible to do for the patient. After the death, he almost always sees a need for supporting the bereaved to accept the altered reality. They need to hear that somebody is talking about the deceased in the past tense and are using words that relate to loss and death. This kind of approach is, according to him, motivated by Christian love to the client and an attempt to help the bereaved come to terms with the loss.

b.   A need to avoid referring to the loss as the bereaved's perceptions are overloaded. The opposite of this approach was presented by a number of civil funeral celebrants in Slovakia, with whom I made contact during my field research at the crematorium. They said that they avoided phrases like death, coffin, etc. because the bereaved had been exposed to them enough during the funeral preparation.

An attempt to not expose the bereaved to expressions which could burden them can be regarded as an expression of sensitivity. At the same time, I am aware of the seriousness of the argument for their use – as a tool for coming to terms with the altered situation. An over-considerate approach can be seen in a different light when we realize that the bereaved go through the process of coming to terms with the situation during the ceremony. Overprotecting them can mean that, although they attend the ceremony, they do not make as much progress with coming to terms with the loss as they could if they had been exposed to a correct level of impulses that could help with the process.[72] On the other hand, this comment does not mean that the grieving can be exposed to any level of burden.

This question cannot be solved without the participation of a psychologist who specializes in the subject of grieving. At the level of a working hypothesis, I hold to the opinion that a minister who is prepared to offer pastoral support during the process of coming to terms with the loss during grieving can do it with the conscious use of these expressions.

2. Coming to terms with changed attitudes to yourself. This area is to a certain extent the consequence of the person's attitude to the loss. Therefore, it is solvable only where the loss has already been processed. If that is not the case, it would be in advance of the impacted person's perceptions of reality – which in the best case might suggest the way out of the situation or in the worst case would not be understandable for the bereaved.

3. Coming to terms with the questions about the implication of the loss for the future. These questions very clearly come to the fore in different situations: for example, where children lose their mother – "Who will look after us?"; when parents lose a young child – "Who will we look after now?"; and when parents lose an adult family member – "We no longer have a dad or a mum."

   A different dimension to the same problem area is experienced when a family through death lose their existing social position, or existing or expected incomes, for example, being unable to repay mortgages, etc. A minister can answer these questions in two ways: (a) entrust the bereaved into God's care and (b) motivate the church community to care for the bereaved.

   a. Entrusting the bereaved into God's care. In cases where this problem is generally noticeable, I recommend that ministers search for homiletical and liturgical opportunities to entrust the bereaved to God's care and homiletically awaken or develop trust in God's care for them.[73]

---

72. Ch. Hürlimann states, "The often highly protective character of our burial forms must make us pause for thought. What is meant here as protection can turn out to be an obstacle in the way that the person grieving should actually go." *Ich will mit dir gehen*, 12.

73. P. Sheppy states, "There is, therefore, the pastoral task of entrusting the mourners to God and of incorporating them into the activity of God in Christ." *Death Liturgy and Ritual, vol. 1*, 60.

    b.   Motivating the church to practical help for the bereaved. The church should express its faith in God in its social attitudes; therefore Filo is correct when he states that "The message should also motivate the church to lovingly serve the specific needs of the bereaved."[74]

Helping to express gratitude for the life of the bereaved. After taking Jenssen into account, the pastoral purpose of the funeral should include "helping the bereaved to give thanks for the life of the deceased."[75] Jenssen regards it as one of the tasks of the pastoral conversation before the funeral and is aware of the difficulties which are connected to this context. Despite the understandable psychological difficulties which, during the period of coming to terms with the loss, hinder the ability to concentrate on experiencing thankfulness,[76] in my opinion ministers should indicate this aspect but not as a required attitude, a dominant experience of thankfulness, but as one of the aims which the bereaved could gradually achieve when processing their grief.

Supporting observations

For the pastoral dimension of funeral sermons, it is important that ministers are able to understand the behaviour of the bereaved and the other members of the congregation during the ceremony. To this end the following observations are included: observations of oscillating emotional stress during the ceremony; the question of crying at the funeral; and a comment about grieving children and answering their questions.

Oscillating emotional stress during the ceremony. When relating to the funeral congregation, the minister needs to know about oscillating emotional stress during the funeral rite. Based on my observations, it is possible to identify two peaks of emotional stress:

- At the closing of the coffin shortly before the start of the funeral, or the drawing of the curtain in the display hall at the crematorium in Banská Bystrica.

---

74. J. Filo, *Evanjeliové možnosti*, 276. He continues, "Based on the gospel commandment to love your neighbour, which is in reality done for Christ ('As you did it to one of the least of these my brothers, you did it to me.' Matt 25:40), in sermons we want to express the love of the church as God's love to the mourning and the desolate."

75. H. H. Jenssen, *Die kirchliche Handlungen*, 189.

76. These psychological difficulties can be made up from the experience of the past as well as the fresh pain of the separation or even a negative assessment of the fate of the bereaved, etc.

- When the coffin is lowered into the grave, or an equivalent act at the crematorium.

These observations can be described in brief. The closing of the coffin brings the realization of the loss because the bereaved think, "I will never see your face again." For the bereaved, the closed coffin becomes a symbol of the deceased person. This is why lowering it into the grave causes a new coming to terms with loss which we can define as thinking, "I will never even see your coffin again." These observations have most significance for funerals where there is a great degree of grief and, to the extent that the liturgy of the church allows it, should be taken into account when the liturgy of the funeral is being determined.[77]

The funeral and crying. Ministers should comfort the bereaved by proclaiming the gospel and thereby assist their processing of their loss and grief. But the processing of loss should also reflect the emotionality of the bereaved who should be able to express their emotions in an authentic way. Ministers therefore must not deliberately induce or block crying.

- Inducing emotions. When evaluating the funeral as a whole, the crying of the most intimately connected bereaved does not have a positive or negative value. It would be completely inappropriate for ministers to deliberately attempt to move the congregation to tears, as if by doing this they achieve an improved expression of the interpersonal ties.[78]
- Blocking emotions. Blocking crying and grieving using the medium of faith is also a very serious mistake because psychologically coming

---

77. I attended the funeral of someone who had committed suicide that had two parts – one in the garden of the grieving family and the other at the graveside. At the part which took place at the graveside, a lay church worker from the church that the parents of the deceased attended gave a comparatively long address. I regarded the content of his address as very good, but for the grieving mother who had to wait an awfully long time for the coffin to be lowered into the ground, I felt the timing of the ceremony was inappropriate. If his address had been included in the part of the funeral in the garden of the grieving family, it could have brought positive stimuli without raising the stress levels of the loved ones.

78. Prof Michalko told his students, "You will quickly find out that it is not hard to make those present cry. But do not do it. That is not the role of a minister." Something similar is stated by I. Kišš: "It is necessary to avoid lamentations not only during the committal but also to not excessively lament about the death during the sermon. We cannot exploit human emotions so that we bring about crying at the funeral. Our aim cannot be to bring the family to tears but we should comfort them. 'Comfort, comfort my people' (Isa 40:1), this is the role of the funeral sermon." *Nádej nad hrobom,* 1, 3.

to terms with the loss does not question the faith of the person facing loss.

Therefore, it can be stated again that crying is not an expression of love that we should try to achieve, nor is it a questioning of faith that we should eliminate. When it spontaneously occurs, it should be regarded as a normal part of the proceedings.

Grieving in children and their "protection" through unanswered questions. An attempt to protect children from stress which they do not understand can lead to an approach that is inappropriate from a long-term point of view. Hürlimann responds to this risk. He states that "The best conditions for the processing of grief in children and later in adults are created where the questions children have regarding dying and death are not rejected – you are too young for that – but they are listened to and discussed."[79] This approach demonstrates that an attempt to protect children must include protecting them in the present moment, as well as in the future, by enabling them to come to terms with stress in a healthy manner.

Luebering is also unequivocally of the opinion that it is necessary to tell children the truth because phrases such as "he departed," or "she is in heaven," or "she is asleep" have different meanings for children which do not correspond to the reality they are experiencing. Each of them describes something that, in terms of a child's experience, is reversible. Therefore, he recommends explaining the physical reality of death using words which the child understands, such as the dead do not breathe. At the same time, he includes arguments in support of his belief that it is better to enable children to attend the funeral ceremony.[80] As in other cases, we also require interdisciplinary help from psychologists as well as from qualified teachers of religious education who have experience with grieving children.

The Evangelistic Aims of Funeral Sermons

In conversations about the evangelistic dimension of funeral sermons, some express the opinion that the funeral sermon is foremost an evangelistic opportunity with other aspects relegated to the background, while others express the opinion that the funeral sermon should not be evangelistic. There

---

79. C. Hürlimann, *Ich will mit dir gehen*, 5.

80. C. Luebering, *Helping a Child Grieve and Grow* (St. Meinrad, IN: Abbey Press, 1990), one of the informative texts from the organization CareNotes.

are good arguments for both of these opposing positions, so it is necessary to seek a balanced approach and attempt to state in what sense the funeral sermon should have, and in what sense it should not have, evangelistic aims. My expression of support for the evangelistic dimension of funeral sermons does not mean an automatic and total agreement with all forms of evangelism in funeral sermons nor with the proportion of the funeral sermon that they take up.

A funeral sermon should have evangelistic aims

I want to introduce my reflections by stating that the Great Commission (Matt 28:18–20) is unambiguously an evangelistic mandate and relates to all the activities of the church. Therefore, based on my overall understanding, funeral sermons must also have an evangelistic dimension which corresponds to the needs of the community.[81] Statistics about the inhabitants of any country suggesting that Christianity is the majority religion do not indicate the real numbers of confessing Christians. In fact they always include a massive number of nominal Christians who do not have a real personal relationship to God and the church. That is why it would be a collective loss for all Christian churches if their ministers did not look for opportunities to invite these people to personal participation in the life of faith in God.

Historical observations about the evangelistic significance of Christian funerals[82] testify that funeral proceedings can have evangelistic potential.[83] These are made even more interesting by the fact that they took place in the period when sermons were not a part of the funeral proceedings. The question

---

81. In contrast to missionary sending there are also missionary needs. For missiological questions, see D. Senior and C. Stuhlmeuller, *The Biblical Foundations for Mission* (City: Orbis, 1983), 372.

82. H. H. Jenssen states, "Emperor Julian the Apostle saw the cause of the unwanted growth of the church, in addition to the hospitality and exemplary lifestyle of Christians in their funeral practice." *Die kirchliche Handlungen*, 179. Similar expectations are observed in later period directly from J. Calvin in his volume on funeral sermons (John Calvin, *Institutes of the Christian Religion*, III, 25.5), and Sheppy comments as follows "Calvin saw the funeral as the pledge of new life, and urged its solemn performance as an occasion in which all bystanders might be reminded of the truth of resurrection and so be shaken out of unbelief" (*Death Liturgy and Ritual, vol. 1*, 95).

83. A disquisition about evangelistic preaching has been produced by J. Vrablec, *Homiletika* (Trnava: SSV, v Cirkevnom nakladateľstve Bratislava, 1987), chapter 2.1: "Misijná kázeň," 24–30.

is whether and to what extent the evangelistic scope of these proceedings is observable today.[84]

In homiletical literature, support for the evangelistic dimension of funeral sermons is expressed, for example, by Josef Smolík who, quoting Seitz, speaks about God whom we encounter in transitional situational occasions,[85] or when Smolík submits the purpose of funeral sermons based on the wording of Mezger, which is directed towards the bringing forth and deepening of faith.[86] In support of proclaiming the Word in transitional situations of life, Elizabeth Kubíková relies on the greater openness of the listeners to hearing the gospel, which she regards as a "great evangelistic opportunity." Therefore, she expects ministers to pay extremely careful attention to the preparation of the sermon.[87] Similarly, Filo states that "God's Word in the funeral sermon and prayers offers witness to the way of salvation prepared by God, which is on the horizon of eternity for all those present."[88]

Agenda ČCE moves the discussion into a critically important deliberation about the evangelistic emphases: (1) a funeral sermon cannot be without evangelistic content and impact, and (2) being evangelistic is not the main purpose of the funeral sermon.[89] They set the purpose as:

1. Catechetical-kerygmatic aim: "strengthen faith in the resurrection"

2. Pastoral aim: "comfort the afflicted"

---

84. The evangelistic scope of the Christian funeral sermon can be demonstrated by the experience of Satyavani, a Christian missionary from India who came from a Hindu family. During her study stay at Belfast Bible College in Belfast in 2008, she described to me how she became a Christian after attending the Christian funeral of her professor.

85. M. Seitz, *Unsere Kasualpraxis – eine gottesdienstliche Gelegenheit* (Praxis des Glaubens, Göttingen: Vandenhoeck and Ruprecht, 1978, 42–50), in J. Smolík, *Radost ze slova*, 149.

86. M. Mezger, *Kasualien* (Evangelisches Kirchenlexikon 3, Vandenhoeck and Ruprecht, 1962, 297) in J. Smolík, *Radost ze slova*, 150: "The aim of funeral preaching can be seen in Mezger's formulation of occasional preaching generally: 'To proclaim and bring as promise one gospel . . . to certain people in their specific situation in order that faith would be brought forth and be deepened . . ., which is hope in temptation, a grasping of our calling in Christ . . . and in this to help people to understand the gospel and with this to saving knowledge of the "individual," in such a way that in their specific life story they could encounter God and they could trust him."

87. J. Kubíková, *Kažte evangelium: metodická pomůcka pro kazatele* (Praha: Blahoslav, 1992), 166.

88. J. Filo, *Evanjeliové možnosti*, 276.

89. *Agenda ČCE*, 195: "Preaching the gospel about the resurrection cannot happen without an evangelistic consideration and impact, even though being evangelistic is not the main aim of a funeral. The aim is to strengthen faith in the resurrection and comfort the afflicted."

Evangelistic "content and impact" are not included in the primary purpose of the funeral sermon, but this agenda counts on the idea that well implemented catechetical-kerygmatic aims and pastoral aims will have an evangelistic impact on the unchurched public. Orthodox authors, Axman and Aleš, regard the funeral sermon as a good opportunity to familiarize the grieving visitors with the eschatological emphasis of the church's doctrine.[90]

Haddon Robinson, based on the state of the bereaved, recommends paying attention to the other members of the funeral congregation, which indirectly leads to a requirement to address the evangelistic emphasis of the funeral sermon.[91] Bryan Chapell sees two basic roles: comforting the bereaved, and reaching people with gospel hope.[92] Preaching the gospel is a legitimate aim of all church preaching; therefore, it should also be regarded as a legitimate aim in funeral preaching. At the same time, a standard part of a church service is each person's response to the Word of God that they have heard. Therefore, a movement towards faith on the basis of what is heard can be regarded as a legitimate part of the proceedings.[93] This still leaves open the question of the method of communication, the method of taking into account the thinking of

---

90. P. O. Axman and P. Aleš state, "In the current circumstances, where the Orthodox church is still in evangelistic conditions, the funeral sermon is a very good opportunity for the minister to briefly familiarize the gathered mourners with the most basic aspects of the faith of the church from the area of eschatology, which is in many elements connected to the overall doctrine of the church." *Homiletika*, 83.

91. H. W. Robinson states, "An implicit assumption here, especially when most of those attending the funeral are not Christians, is that the preacher is not speaking primarily to the immediate family. Their current grief probably causes them not to hear what the preacher has to say at this moment. That does not mean that we should try to speak a few words of comfort, but primarily I'm going to speak to the extended friends and family who are there." H. W. Robinson, J. E. Means, and P. D. Borden, "Guidelines for Difficult Funerals," in *Contemporary Handbook*, eds. A. Malphurs and K. Willhite, 211, fn. 3.

92. Chapell states, "Comfort and reach with gospel hope." Apart from a positively expressed aim, he also adds a negatively expressed aim: "Do not berate or lecture." *Christ-Centered Preaching*, 344.

93. J. Hrdlička notes this reality in Rahner and describes it as follows: According to Rahner, in transcendental theology it is *Gotteserfahren* when God existentially touches man, who feels that he is confronted with the mystery of his being and his responsibility for it and also with that which is behind everything, and at the same time he knows that God exists and is with him and in gentle, omniscient and patient dialogue. The person remains completely free for this experience to become a spiritual turning point or he can completely destroy and deny it. *Stručná homiletika* (Olomouc: MCM, 1991), 25–26, quoted in P. Zemko, *Homiletické směrnice. Z dějin homiletiky na Moravě, v Čechách a na Slovensku* (Trnava: Dobrá kniha, 2007), 79.

the listeners and how to create the space for an authentic response. This applies both for the majority population as well as funerals for minority groups.[94]

Sugden and Wiersbe also rely on the evangelistic dimension of funeral sermons. They motivate ministers with the words: "Deal with the great truths of the gospel. . . . Your gracious handling of the funeral service could give you opportunity to minister to the family later and perhaps reach them for Christ and the church."[95]

This suggested approach brings to the evangelistic dimension of funeral sermons a trust in God and relies on his working during the funeral ceremony and in the future. This lowers the pressure of making an instant decision and provides more freedom for both ministers and the bereaved. Ministers are liberated from disproportionate pressure and anxiety that the opportunity for evangelism is "now or never." An appropriate and well conducted funeral ceremony supports the bereaved in their time of crisis. Building on this experience requires further pastoral-evangelistic contact with the bereaved which allows them to come to terms with the gospel in such a time frame as corresponds to their mental and spiritual processing.

In my opinion, this is an appropriate approach, but it is only feasible in an environment where the minister is able to allocate enough time for friendships and pastoral visits. The question is how can this complex message be communicated to the listeners in an understandable and credible way? It is not about "evangelism" in terms of the statistical growth of a given community, the realization of the aims of that community, but it is about evangelism as service: through faith in Christ, people can resolve their metaphysical questions and improve the quality of their life. This kind of evangelistic understanding should be primarily addressed to those without Christian faith and lead to the

---

94. An important aspect is taking into account the specifics of various cultures in preaching, as well as the principles of inter-cultural communication of the gospel. The issue of Roma culture in homiletical activity in the church is indicated in V. Šoltésová, "Využitie rómskeho prekladu Písma v homiletickej činnosti cirkví na východnom Slovensku," in *Homiletická činnosť cirkví a kvalita súčasného života. Zborník prednášok z vedeckej teologickej konferencie* (Banská Bystrica: KETM PF UMB a ZEC vo vyd. Trian, p. r. o., 2009), 128–134.

95. H. F. Sugden and W. W. Wiersbe, *Confident Pastoral Leadership*, 106. Through a christological emphasis, Rummage also supports the missionary dimension of funeral sermons when he states that funerals belong to the opportunities where the minister addresses the largest group of people, and at these occasions there is often a larger number of non-Christians than at an ordinary church service. Therefore, he recommends preaching in such a way that the minister directs the listeners to Jesus Christ, and he continues: "All of the biblical themes associated with . . . funeral sermons can be readily connected to faith in God's Son. We should find opportunities to focus on Jesus throughout the sermon and to proclaim the redemption available through faith in Christ." S. N. Rummage, "Redemptive Sermons," 651.

growth of God's kingdom. Numerical growth of the church that the minister who conducts the ceremony belongs to is, from this perspective, a secondary issue. Ministers do indeed expect that people who open up to the faith will look to develop their spiritual lives in the church where they belong, but this should not exclude joy when, under the influence of their sermon, a formal member of another church deepens devotion and approaches God based on the ways and doctrines of their church.

The deformation of the evangelistic aims of funeral sermons

After expressing support for the idea that funeral sermons should have an evangelistic dimension, I must warn about a number of potential problems: (1) reducing the purpose of a funeral sermon to only evangelism; (2) inadequate evangelistic assumptions; and (3) inadequate evangelistic practice.

1. Reducing the purpose of a funeral sermon to only evangelism. My observations of funeral sermons demonstrate that ministers who attempt to include an evangelistic emphasis in their preaching inadequately combine the reality of the loss with the evangelistic dimension of their ministry. This occurs because of the following:

    a. The view that there are two alternatives – that a sermon can be only either pastoral or evangelistic.

    b. Not sufficiently taking the homiletical situation into account. This is why there is an inadequate combining of the reality of loss and the evangelistic dimension of the sermon.

    c. Inability or unacceptability of applying the gospel to the pastoral message of the funeral sermon.

    The consequences of this approach can be found in the following areas:

    - *An absence of pastoral support for the grieving.* If the purpose of funeral sermons is reduced to only evangelism, it is not a true evangelism. This kind of deformed "mission" has to be regarded as either a mistake or an abuse of evangelistic elements as a hiding place from the stress arising from the challenges of this ministry.

      In contrast, when the message is connected to the homiletical situation and has a strong pastoral message, then the evangelistic dimension of the ministry develops without a direct evangelistic message. When the bereaved can perceive the strength of faith in their particular life crisis, or when this possibility is demonstrated in an understandable and culturally relevant way, then the funeral sermon cannot remain without an evangelistic influence on the rest of those in attendance.

- *It calls into question ministers' understanding of the gospel.* Ministers who only concentrate on evangelistic emphases indicate that they do not understand the gospel. If they understood it, they would be able to express its meaning for the deceased and the bereaved and its meaning as a support for coming to terms with the process of grieving from the perspective of the Christian faith. Ministers would be able to demonstrate that on the basis of the gospel that we have a life that finds stability in Christ.

- *Doubting the gospel itself.* In a funeral sermon which calls listeners to faith, there should be the possibility to see the relevance of the gospel. But if people observe that those who are preaching the gospel do not have the courage to combine it with the real struggles of life, then they will come to the conclusion that it is only applicable to "recruitment drives" but not to life itself. If at the same time listeners see that ministers behave in a dignified and trustworthy way, they will not doubt them but will doubt the gospel itself. Therefore, I regard concentrating only on evangelistic aspects as not only a bad theological conclusion, but the outcome is that the gospel is doubted. This occurs when *formal* Christocentricity is developed, but it is not developed into *functional* Christocentricity. If the priest is unable to demonstrate the relationship of Christ to the situation, how can those attending the funeral be expected to do it?

- *The loss of a message in certain cases.* The problem of reducing the aims of a funeral sermon to only one – evangelism – can be clearly recognized if we imagine a small funeral where a minister is burying an active Christian surrounded by a small circle of active Christians. For this kind of funeral congregation, the minister needs to be able to preach a funeral sermon. But if the minister only knows an evangelistic emphasis, then the minister does not have anything to offer and remains helpless because this emphasis is inappropriate for the circumstances.

2. Inadequate evangelistic assumptions. Primarily this is ministers being limited to their own church tradition and doubting the faith of

other Christians. The evangelistic activity of the church should call non-Christians to live in community with Christ, which is expressed by joining a particular church community. If ministers do not make it clear that there are two levels to the decision process,[96] they give the impression to Christians from other churches that they are part of the mission field. I hold the opinion that this kind of approach is a mistake because even in the case of a "success," it would only lead to the statistical growth of the community of the given minister, but it would have no significance for the growth of the church of Christ.[97]

The problem of a decreased tolerance to other forms of Christianity is not only encountered in the activities of small radical groups, but it frequently develops in large communities where one Christian church strongly dominates. Anyone who does not belong to that church can be regarded as part of a sect. According to a documentary on a national Slovak TV channel, this was the experience of Roman Catholic missionaries in the former USSR in areas dominated by the Orthodox church.

Christian proclamation of the Word should expound the truth of God's Word and "bring about the obedience of faith for the sake of his name among all the nations" (Rom 1:5). When doing this, ministers should proceed very sensitively, especially in situations where there is the danger of opening a doctrinal dispute, because it is unwise to include polemical or offensive thoughts in a funeral sermon.[98] People who are confronting a loss should not be burdened with further problems. Ministers who struggle for the truth of the Word must in this case show a greater reliance on the transcendental

---

96. For a life of faith and for an expression of faith in the tradition of a certain church.

97. During my studies at the theological seminary of the Evangelical Free Church in German Democratic Republic (Buckow, Märkische Schweiz), one of the guest lecturers clearly expressed the pointlessness of this proselytizing from the perspective of God's kingdom by taking five marks from one of his pockets and putting them into the other. He commented, "Think about how much richer I have become!"

98. Lloyd M. Perry expresses a different opinion. "If there had been any special circumstances in connection with the life, they should be used as a point of interest that can be made to lead to the truth." That he is thinking about the bereaved is demonstrated by the choice of the following illustration: "For example, if the deceased was a Christian and had Roman Catholic relatives and friends, emphasize well (by backing it up with sufficient Scripture) that the deceased didn't go to purgatory but to be with Christ." *A Manual for Biblical Preaching* (Grand Rapids: Baker, 1992), 189.

power of God's activity. Therefore, they can in faith renounce criticism of the doctrinal positions of other churches.

3.   Inadequate evangelistic practice.

- An abuse of power. A funeral sermon cannot be "evangelistic" in the sense that those present must hear and agree. In our exegesis of Matthew 28:18–20, we must search for what the Greek word *mathēteusate* means in relationship to an expression of power to the target group.[99] The translation, "make disciples," used in Roháčk's Slovak Bible translations (and most English Bibles) does not sufficiently take into account the will of the individual and can lead to justification of tactlessness on behalf of the Christian. The Slovak ecumenical translation of "win disciples" shows more sensitivity to the reaction of the people addressed and does not give Christians the feeling of having the right to use excessive pressure to achieve a holy aim.

- If ministers are to win disciples for Christ, their task is clearly defined: they should proclaim God's Word. They must deliver it in such a way that listeners can think and not feel the need to become defensive. Therefore, all forms of pressure which do not give listeners the space to independently come to terms with the offer of the gospel, and instead force them to defend themselves, must be regarded as being damaging to the gospel.

- A loss of power. If it is true that a funeral sermon cannot put pressure on people, it must also be said that it is a mistake if the minister loses the courage to address the funeral congregation evangelistically after observing its misuse. Shortcomings cannot be repaired by eliminating the phenomenon as a whole but by searching for appropriate methods.

For these reasons, I hold the opinion we cannot diminish the evangelistic dimension of the funeral sermon. Simultaneously, I stand against simplified

---

99. J. P. Louw and Eugene Albert Nida (eds.) recommend that when translating into national languages that expressions are chosen that do not create the impression of a denial of free response of those being addressed. As appropriate methods, they state, "convince them to become my disciples" or "urge them to be my disciples." In rendering *mathēteuō* in Matt 28:19 and similar contexts, it is important to avoid the implication of duress or force, that is to say, one should not translate "force them to be my disciples" or "compel them to be my disciples." This might very well be implied in a literal translation of a causative such as "to make." *Greek-English Lexicon of the New Testament: Based on Semantic Domain, vol. 1* (New York: United Bible Societies, 1999), 471.

attempts at fulfilling the evangelistic dimension, because even the Great Commission (Matt 28:18–20) should not be applied mechanically and inadequately, and I stand against doubting God's activity with Christians from other Christian traditions. This demonstrates that it is not possible to fulfil the evangelistic aspects of a funeral sermon with stereotypical and routine approaches. Listeners will quickly recognize whether ministers are standing there as a witness to faith or if they are only mechanically reproducing "what they must say regardless." Based on this observation, the listeners will decide if they will pay attention. Ministers are potentially limiting the reach of their work.

Combining the pastoral and evangelistic aims

Dividing the purpose of funeral sermons into pastoral and evangelistic is only a learning tool. This can be seen in Mezger's understanding of situational preaching as an aid to the understanding of a person's own life,[100] and this is clearly not in the sense of finding an answer to why it happened – justification of the loss – but more in the sense of understanding the existence of humans in connection with their existence before God. Josef Smolík applies this general definition of the aim of situational preaching from Mezger to the conditions of funeral preaching and demonstrates two theological aims, which are interconnected and have a tendency towards going deeper:

1. An encounter with God, meaning a mediated encounter with God in the specific life situation of the grieving.

2. Trust in God, meaning not just any kind of encounter but an encounter which leads to an ability to trust God.[101]

So it is appropriate to examine whether there are factors that actively support the achievement of this aim but also if there are those that prevent or make it difficult to achieve the aim. In summary, it is possible to say that both aims are about the beginning or the support of faith for use in everyday life.

---

100. M. Mezger, *Kasualien* (Evangelisches Kirchenlexikon 3, Vandenhoeck and Ruprecht, 1962), 297, quoted in Smolík, *Radost ze Slova*, 150: "To help the person to understand the gospel and by this to a saving knowledge of the 'case,' so that in their own life stories they could meet with God and they could trust in him."

101. J. Smolík, *Radost ze Slova*, 150.

4

The Homiletical Process

If it is true that a funeral sermon is "a sermon including everything that goes with it,"[1] then the homiletical process used in preparing this situational sermon must take into account all the stages of homiletical work. Support for this position comes from Elizabeth Kubíková when she contends that all the rules of homiletics apply when preparing a situational sermon.[2] These sermons are different from the proclamation of the Word at a regular church service because ministers, after a certain time, know their own church congregation and are able to take into consideration the homiletical situation without needing to consciously define the individual traits. This however may not apply to funeral sermons. In the case of the deceased and their social circle, the homiletical situation can be significantly altered. Therefore, ministers need to pay appropriate attention to it.

The Stages of Preparing a Funeral Sermon

It is possible to divide the stages of preparing a funeral sermon as follows: (1) collecting source material; (2) choosing the biblical text; (3) working with the text (exegesis); (4) applying the text to the situation of the listeners (homiletical meditation); and (5) stylizing the sermon.

This means that the preparation of a funeral sermon requires all the application of the standard stages of the homiletical process. The difference may be in the apparent tension which arises from the fact that during their preparation, ministers must keep the message as their objective priority and investigating the homiletical situation as their time priority. Only by doing this

---

1. J. Filo, *Evanjeliové možnosti*, in J. Filo, *Pohľady do neba*, 276.
2. J. Kubíková, *Kažte evangelium*, 165.

can they find a message for the situation, if they know the situation, and only doing this prevent the biblical message from becoming secondary.

Collecting Source Material

In chapter 2 on the homiletical situation of a funeral, the areas of which a minister needs to be pastorally aware are listed, and they form the foundations for the preparation of the funeral sermon. Therefore, we know "what" we need to find out. The question remains "how" to find it out. Ministers can find the answers during pastoral contact with the family after the death of the deceased; in conversation with trustworthy members of the church; in their own notes from pastoral visits; and based on being inspired during conversations with members of the local community.

Pastoral contact with the family after the death of the deceased
One of the opportunities for gaining valuable source material is the timely personal contact between ministers and the bereaved after the death. It should be regarded as an irreplaceable part of pastoral ministry and the basis of the pastoral context of the proclamation of the gospel at the funeral service.[3] This contact can occur in the minister's office, but based on my experience, it is much better if the minister visits the grieving in their own homes. In smaller churches this pastoral visit generally occurs immediately after the minister learns of the death, either from the bereaved or another member of the church. It is also described as happening this way by Catholic or Lutheran ministers of smaller parishes. As far as the timing of this visit is concerned, according to Sugden and Wiersbe, it is not necessary to take into consideration the time of day: "We may set hours for counselling people but not for comforting people."[4] According to them, pastoral sensitivity should be shown not only by being prepared to visit, but also by telephoning to "see if a visit is in order."[5]

---

3. Similarly, H. H. Jenssen states, "A pastoral conversation with the bereaved is a prerequisite of a funeral sermon." *Die kirchliche Handlungen*, in *Handbuch der Praktischen Theologie*, vol. 2, 189.

4. H. F. Sugden and W. W. Wiersbe, *Confident Pastoral Leadership*, 103.

5. Ibid.

The aim of pastoral contact before the funeral

Regardless of the manner of death,[6] it is possible to divide the aims of pastoral contact with the bereaved into two groups: (a) pastoral support and (b) gaining source material and inspiration for the preparation of the funeral sermon.

a) Pastoral support. Even though the pastoral contact with the bereaved is primarily being mentioned in connection with situational homiletics, ministers must conduct this visit as pastoral crisis intervention and not only as an administrative task to gain details for the funeral. They should be with the bereaved so that they are not alone in their loss, and provide them with pastoral support. If the bereaved are able to communicate, they often recall the final moments of the deceased's life and speak about what this person meant to them. They recall many details, for example how the deceased looked at them for the last time, what the deceased said, and what they thought. Sometimes the bereaved repeat information they have already given. This type of conversation is not informative, but it is a form of processing an extremely stressful experience. To inexperienced ministers, this information might seem useless, and they might think that they could make better use of their time. But this kind of evaluation would be a serious mistake. A sensible amount of contact with the bereaved is one of the best ways ministers can invest their time.

According to Jenssen, ministers can quickly enter into a deeper conversation by briefly discussing the liturgical form of the funeral with the bereaved.[7] In this way, ministers can learn more about the characteristic personality traits of the bereaved as well as the depth of their interpersonal relationships.

If the bereaved are incapable of conversation or even taking part in prayers (this is generally connected to the manner of death or personality types) – even then the presence of the minister has value as pastoral support, and this experience can be beneficial in the search for a biblical message for the funeral sermon.[8]

---

6. Differences arise due to a number of perspectives: manner of death, intensity of the shock, ability or inability of the bereaved to communicate with the minister, etc. A particular set of differences arise depending on whether the minister knows or does not know the deceased and the bereaved. Therefore, I recommend that that minister pays special attention to the theoretical preparation of this type of pastoral visit.

7. H. H. Jenssen, *Die kirchliche Handlungen*, 189.

8. Sugden and Wiersbe recommend that the minister, at an appropriate moment, offer a reading from the Bible and a prayer. In this they clearly warn, "[A]nd please do this with heart! A perfunctory reading of the Word, followed by a routine prayer, will only make the wounds hurt more. Ask God to give you a heart of compassion." *Confident Pastoral Leadership*, 103.

b) Gaining source material for the funeral sermon. Even though it is a pastoral visit in the fullest sense of the word, the minister is simultaneously gaining ideas for the preparation of the funeral sermon. Ministers need to know the family for whom they will conduct the funeral in order to set appropriate homiletical aims and in the message, to react to the specific situation of the family afflicted by loss. If ministers underestimate the importance of observing the loss and investigating the religious potential for accepting the message, it can, according to Jenssen, lead to the promise of eternal life being proclaimed ineffectively. But it also shows that "to know" the bereaved means to know their religious beliefs and to search for appropriate ways to connect to them in the message.[9] Because of this, ministers also need to listen to the members of the grieving family. They can learn about who the deceased was for them. It is appropriate to notice what the relatives are saying, but also what they avoid. Carr recommends discerning tensions and conflicts and constructing a rough grid of the relationships which can help ministers to understand the grief in a particular case.[10] After this kind of visit, it is obvious to ministers that they cannot fulfil their task by simply declaring general religious ideas. They are thinking about real people and need to ask the question, "What can I do for you?" It is surprising how many important ideas ministers can obtain, even from families they have known for many years.

Contact with the bereaved can also expose ministers to inappropriate requests. Orthodox authors, Axman and Aleš, state that, "Sometimes the bereaved attempt to directly impose their ideas about what should be said about the deceased on the priest (they may even write the sermon). The minister should only choose verified and objective information and not give in to the temptation to give the sermon a non-biblical focus!"[11]

Conversations with trustworthy members of the church

The personal experience of individual members of the church often does not provide ministers with an adequate picture of the person. If ministers are new to the church, their short-term experiences with the deceased could

---

9. H. H. Jenssen, *Die kirchliche Handlungen*, 189.

10. W. Carr states, "To facilitate this process, the minister needs to listen when he meets the relatives of the deceased, and especially members of the wider family. If he can begin to discern tensions and conflicts, as well as expressions of hope and unsuspected affection, he may be able to construct in his own mind a rough grid of relationships and so place the deceased in it. This will assist him to imbue the formality of grieving in the course of the funeral with necessary reality." *Brief Encounters*, 112.

11. P. O. Axman and P. Aleš, *Homiletika*, 83.

be completely different from the lifelong experiences of their neighbours or colleagues.[12] Therefore I recommend that, as soon as ministers start in a new positon, they begin to form functioning relationships with the members of the church board, presbyters, or elders on whom they can rely when they need to learn information about the person they are about to bury. In society at large, there is a strongly established notion of "not speaking ill of the dead." Therefore, ministers must warn those with this tendency that concealing important negative facts can distort the work of the sermon, which can also be damaging to the church. Of course, ministers cannot use this information arbitrarily, and they must not use it as an end in itself during the funeral sermon.

Notes from previous pastoral visits

Klaus Fuhrmann recommended to his students another area for gaining source materials for funeral sermons.[13] He advised them that after normal pastoral visits to the seriously ill or elderly church members, they maintain a card index with notes. Only a few people are able to remember for a long time minor details that are for them insignificant but are important to the other person. But in this way ministers can store this information in order to personalize that person's funeral. It will be a great help in preparing the sermon if ministers can look up specific sections of conversations with the deceased, their memories, favourite Bible verse, etc. I can also recommend this advice as being methodologically correct and ethically sound, but ministers must not forget that it would be an unnecessary stress for the dying who are still battling with illness or the bereaved if they knew or sensed that a minister had recorded a comment for possible use at the funeral.

Other opportunities

Ministers must also take into account other information from their social surroundings. The reaction of the community to the news of the death helps

---

12. An older minister once told me that he had entered the ceremonial room where he was to bury an elderly gentleman, whom he had regarded as a good Christian. On the coffin, he reportedly found a note that read: "This devil should have been here ages ago."

13. A teacher of practical theology at the seminary Freier Evangelischer Gemeinden, Buckow, German Democratic Republic. I was taught by Fuhrmann in the school year 1983/84. In a certain sense, Sugden and Wiersbe go even further when they recommend that ministers pray about the message for the funeral when an older member of their church is hospitalized or is terminally ill. This approach they recommend especially for those regarded as "pillars of the church." *Confident Pastoral Leadership*, n. 106.

add in picturing the deceased and helps create a broader, more anchored image – which improves the preaching ministry.

Helpful for proclamation, or a waste of time?

Details and observations that ministers gain in contact with the bereaved and from other sources form the foundational starting point for their preparation of the funeral. Reflecting on this information provides ministers with criteria to judge the appropriateness of the biblical text on which they want to preach and gives them some direction when defining the objective of their work. The significance of this approach cannot be evaluated by "the number of lines" gained for the funeral sermon. The opposite is in fact true – knowing the context is essential, even when the minister decides not to include it in the wording of the sermon.

This approach provides the following benefits for the homiletic process:

1. Pastoral boundaries to the homiletical proceedings. The funeral ceremony will not come across to the bereaved as an impersonal liturgical-homiletical act which is conducted for them "contractually" by unknown ministers, but it becomes a ceremony in which ministers who pray for them have already expressed that they are there for them in their loss. This is significant for members of the church, and also for people who are not a part of the church, because through this contact there may be opportunity for sensitive evangelistic conversations in the future.

2. The possibility for non-verbal communication of gospel attitudes. If a minister is available for the bereaved in the time immediately after their loss, at that moment it is not the minister's words that are most important, but the minister's presence. In this way, ministers demonstrate God's love in the form of human concern for those who are suffering.

3. An increased forthrightness to the message and increasing its impact. The correct understanding of the bereaved's situation and their needs can influence the minister when choosing the text and writing the sermon, which can result in a more powerful impact.

4. Supporting the authenticity of ministers. As they know, or get to know, the bereaved, it reduces their natural tendency to hide behind a "professional" style. Therefore, the funeral ceremony itself will be

much more personal and will be less stressful for ministers, even though empathy may bring its own burdens.[14]

Choosing the Text for the Sermon

Is a text for a funeral sermon necessary? The Bible should be the starting point of a Christian ceremony as well as the content of the sermon. Sometimes this position is questioned. Ján Jaminský, from a historical perspective, observes and criticizes the trend that started in the second half of the nineteenth century for the Bible to be used less and less in funeral sermons. It arises from the view that the text is not essential, so that it is not a prerequisite for a sermon.[15] He takes a clear stand against this view and states that "a sermon, whose task it is to bring the church before God, does not exist without the word which God gives to his community, which also cannot exist without the text."[16] His starting point is the irreplaceability of the Word of God. The minister therefore, according to Ján Jaminský, cannot reduce the text to a source of ideas but must understand it as God's activity and as his gracious Word.

At the current time the question of the necessity for and the suitability of the biblical text for the funeral sermon must also be addressed. Axman and Aleš state that "It is not correct to choose as the topic of the coffin side farewell a statement of the deceased and then with eulogizing words convey and comment on it." This approach would lead to a "degradation of the words of the gospel."[17] This is why they recommend that "A sermon must be based on the Holy Bible at all times, as the gospel of salvation must be preached everywhere."[18] Kubíková holds a similar opinion – the situational sermon "must be based on the biblical text."[19]

---

14. A minister needs to develop the ability to empathize but at the same time not to transfer that information to areas which shouldn't be burdened by it.

15. J. Jamnický, *Evanjelické pohrebné kázne,* 94; he continues, "This was once the opinion of the Frenchman, A. Vinet, then Claud Harms, M. Baumgarten, I. R. Hanny and others producing adequate scientific replicas (K. I. Nitzsch, Jul. Müller, H. Weiss). The practical applicability of this opinion of sermons without a text is rarely put to the test as it is very characteristic that actually those that held this opinion very rarely completely put this starting point into practice; for example, Claud Harms only preached a few times without a text."

16. Ibid., 96.

17. P. O. Axman and P. Aleš, *Homiletika,* 83.

18. Ibid., 82.

19. J. Kubíková, *Kažte evangelium,* 165.

Jamincký provides a number of reasons for a sermon text from theological and communicative perspectives. In his view, taking the biblical text as the starting point expresses the dependence of the minister and the listeners on God's revelation in the Bible; the desire and expectation of the Christian church that God's Word be preached to them and not the minister's theological doctrine; a protection against jumbled ideas – the text limits the content of the sermon which helps to make it understandable and memorable; and encouragement to ministers to be disciplined in their thinking.[20]

The options for choosing the sermon text

The biblical text is the starting point for a funeral sermon as well as giving it life. This means that we must find a way of choosing a suitable text. A warning against inappropriate expectations is provided by Jenssen's opinion that, in relation to choosing the text for the funeral sermon, it is not possible to formulate universally valid recommendations because of the diverse lives people live.[21] But Rudolf Bohren emphasizes that the text for a funeral sermon should be chosen in consideration of the particular situation,[22] and it is possible to find support for this approach in church guidelines about funeral ceremonies.[23]

When choosing the text of the sermon, there are essentially two options: (1) Accepting texts that are set in some way; and (2) ministers make their own choice.

1) Accepting set texts, for example Sunday lectionary reading, or the text from confirmation. Smolík and Jamnický both advise ministers to use texts from Sunday, which provide ample material because it is supposedly good when the funeral sermon is connected to the Word the congregation heard

20. J. Jamnický, *Evanjelické pohrebné kázne*, 95.

21. Ibid.

22. R. Bohren, *Predigtlehre*, 38. Against this, K. Dirshaue warns about the very *serious* fact that "songs, psalms, readings and sermon are set by the church. Therefore, these elements should not one-sidedly relate to the case but should be determined by the church year. With this the case is liberated from becoming too conspicuous." This comment refers to the very serious reality – the church service congregation (church) – and it would be a pity if, due to focusing on the deceased, the significance of the church service community was overlooked. *Der totgeschwiegene Tod*, 165, quoted in Ch. Stebler, *Die drei Dimensionen*, 28.

23. For example, the funeral guidelines of the Roman Catholic Church in Slovakia (SSV 2008) have a section on choosing the biblical text, where it recommends appropriate texts based on the case of the deceased. The guidelines for the Lutheran church contain something similar as they provide a broad range of appropriate texts for particular types of deaths.

the previous Sunday.[24] Jamnický sees the benefit of this advice to be that it unburdens ministers from searching for an appropriate text.

But in terms of disadvantages, he presents three problems: the funeral sermon sounds general without personalized remarks; the risk of lazy, unconscientious reproduction of the Sunday sermon; and abusing and distorting the texts.[25] Jamnický is also critical of using a text from a confirmation or a wedding when burying a person.[26] I lean towards being critical of the notion of using the texts from Sunday as the starting point for the funeral sermon. But if the texts from Sunday are actually appropriate for the funeral sermon, it is possible to use them, because ministers have already done their exegesis, and those listening to the sermon can create a link between the church service proclamation of the gospel and their own life situation. But this approach cannot be universally recommended as some "Sunday texts" open questions that are different from the questions addressed in a funeral sermon.

Another type of "set text" is the request that is occasionally made by the bereaved or the dying person that the minister would preach on a text that had significant meaning for them, or a text that they chose as the basis for their funeral sermon.[27] Sugden and Wiersbe have the same train of thought when they directly recommend ministers to ask if the deceased or the bereaved have a favourite passage of Scripture.[28] With this method of choosing the text for the sermon, ministers are able to preach on a text that is significant for the people in question. A risk of this approach is that ministers may receive a text that does not enable the fulfilment of the purpose of a funeral sermon.

2) Ministers make their own choice. As a part of this option, "the first hermeneutical decision to be made is the selection of texts, which is usually determined on a pre-critical basis . . . of intuition that these texts will speak to the congregation under these specific circumstances."[29] When I analyzed the relationship between the particular case and the text of the sermon in the funeral sermons of Prof Igor Kišš, I made extensive observations about the

---

24. J. Smolík, *Radost ze slova*, 150. Jamnický, *Evanjelické pohrebné kázne*, 102.

25. J. Jamnický, *Evanjelické pohrebné kázne*, 102.

26. Ibid.

27. I encountered this kind of request from someone who had been ill for a long time and was terminally ill. During a series of pastoral visits, he requested a number of times that at his funeral I would preach on a certain text. As the text was appropriate for a funeral sermon, I respected his wishes.

28. H. F. Sugden and W. W. Wiersbe, *Confident Pastoral Leadership*, 104.

29. J. A. Melloh, "Homily or Eulogy?," 508.

options for choosing the text of the sermon.[30] The results can be summarized as follows. Ministers can choose the text in two ways: (1) considering the differentiation;[31] and (2) without considering the differentiation.[32]

1. When choosing based on a consideration of the differentiation, it is possible to choose the text in several ways:

   a. In accordance with the differentiation. When choosing the text of the sermon in accordance with the differentiation, ministers can decide as follows:

   To choose a text for the sermon based on a similar situation in the Bible, when ministers find certain features of the case in the biblical text. An example of such a choice is the selection of 2 Samuel 18:33 for a funeral after the tragic death of a young son, because the minister sees features of the current case in the biblical story about David's grief after the tragic death of Absalom. This choice can be evaluated positively: if the minister provides an opportunity to biblically understand the case, and in certain cases this enables the expression of pain and grief; or negatively: it can be often seen that this text does not provide the stimuli for textually achieving the homiletical aims which the minister needs to set. The minister then requires additional biblical texts or attempts to complete the roles of the funeral sermon without connecting it to the text of the sermon.

   To choose a text for the sermon based on the similarity of the ideas. Ministers do not search for similarities between the case and the text on the level of formal parallels, but search for them on the level of a shift in the meaning of the term. For example, after the sudden death of a bus driver from a heart attack, the minister decides to choose a text on the basis of a term that is typical for the deceased to use, such as "way." In the form of a text for the sermon, the minister transforms it to the kerygmatic level. Due to the idea of being on the way to eternity,

---

30. A. Masarik, *Analýza nekérygmatických komponentov pohrebných*, 28–44.

31. Differentiation is understood in Protestant situational homiletics as being the basic features of the case of the deceased. For more details about differentiation, see Masarik, *Analýza nekérygmatických komponentov pohrebných*, 15–27. About choosing the text of the sermon based on a consideration of the differentiation, see 29–42.

32. About choosing the text of the sermon without considering the differentiation see ibid., 43–44.

the minister chooses the text John 14:4: "And you know the way to where I am going." By doing this, the minister has an excellent possibility for Christocentric preaching.

A different possibility is searching for a biblical evaluation of the dominant features of the deceased. At the funeral of a man who was gifted and used it to serve his neighbours, the minister analyzed the features of the case and came to the conclusion that the deceased received his gifting from God and with the fact that he used it; he was a good steward of the talents God had given him. Therefore, the minister decided to use the text of Matthew 25:20–21: "And he who had received the five talents came forward, bringing five talents more, saying, 'Master, you delivered to me five talents; here, I have made five talents more.' His master said to him, 'Well done, good and faithful servant. You have been faithful over a little; I will set you over much. Enter into the joy of your master.'"

On the basis of my observations, I can say that at the funeral of a mature Christian, ministers do not have to run only to formal Christocentricity, but they can show Christ also by looking at the impact of his work in the life of the deceased.

To choose a text for the sermon on the basis of using the Bible as a descriptor. Ministers sometimes look for possibilities to express observations about the pain of the one dying or the bereaved, not by using sentences filled with emotion, but by finding in the Bible a testimony or at least a section of a testimony which can be used as a descriptor to express the difficulty of the situation. An example of this approach is the funeral of a middle-aged woman who died from a serious case of cancer. The minister, by his choice of text, wanted to express the suffocating burden the deceased had to go through: "the sun's light failed" (Luke 23:45).

With this kind of choice, it is impossible to speak about a text for the sermon in the proper sense. It is only a tool which is used to attempt to describe the situation of the deceased and the bereaved. It is not a text for a sermon because in it we do not find a message that would fulfil the purpose of a funeral sermon. Therefore, I regard this choice of text as disadvantageous. If ministers for some reason needed to quote this text, they could use it as a secondary text rather than as the primary text of the sermon. For that role, they should have chosen a text that provides a sufficient amount of inspiration to fulfil the purpose of a funeral sermon.

b.   As a counterpoint to the differentiation, in which case ministers can decide to choose something . . .

  i.   Which appears to be a counterpoint to the differentiation. This kind of choice was made at the funeral of a lonely, widowed, elderly gentleman where the minister chose Proverbs 23:18 as the text for the sermon: "Surely there is a future, and your hope will not be cut off." This approach from a superficial evaluation, or if the homiletical process is biased, may appear to be just religious language with no relationship to reality. But if it is well processed, it can create the space for a powerful testimony to faith – God gives hope even where from a non-religious point of view it would not be expected. I only recommend this approach to ministers who combine high quality biblical-exegetical work with an attitude of testifying to the faith as a minister of the Bible. I do not recommend it for ministers who are in a critical period in their personal faith life because their non-verbal communication can seriously influence the whole communication process and their preaching.

  ii.   Which is a real counterpoint. Igor Kišš kept his principle of not directly rebuking when choosing the text for a middle-aged alcoholic who died in mysterious circumstances (sermon no. 38). In this case, he could have searched for a text of rebuke, but instead he chose a text which was a counterpoint to the situation as it speaks about searching for good: Jeremiah 6:16b, "Ask . . . where the good way is; and walk in it, and find rest for your souls." From the thought process of the sermon, it is clear that the minister did not want to avoid the problems in the life of the deceased, but he did not need to detail them. He spoke about the mistakes of people, and those present knew it was also about the mistakes of the deceased. The text itself speaks about walking the good way. The admonishment was not based on moralizing from the minister, but from the Bible. Therefore, this relationship between the differentiation and the text can be regarded as being pastorally sensitive and appropriate for achieving the aims of the funeral sermon.

When observing the choice of a text that is a real counterpoint to the differentiation, I discovered that, for the funerals of complicated cases, ministers do not have to choose to make a direct rebuke. They can also achieve the same impact by choosing a text that is a counterpoint to the differentiation, which is pastorally sensitive, more culturally acceptable, and provides the basis for effective proclamation of the Word.

c.   Choosing a text to communicate with those attending.[33] A wide range of possibilities of texts can be chosen. There are texts which express their message in the form of:

i.   God's words. In a text for a sermon that expresses its message in the form of a quote from God, we can find a number of different recipients.

God's Word to the departing. At the funeral of a man about age sixty, the minister chose the text 2 Corinthians 12:9: "My grace is sufficient for you." Everyone lives before God, and he has something to say about our existence. This does not apply only for the one departing but for us all generally. If ministers make use of the ideas in this choice, they establish a foundation for preaching effectively.

God's testimony about the deceased. At the funeral of a devout elderly woman during Christmas, the minister chose the text of Revelation 14:13: "And I heard a voice from heaven saying, 'Write this: Blessed are the dead who die in the Lord from now on.' 'Blessed indeed,' says the Spirit, 'that they may rest from their labours, for their deeds follow them.'" The minister wanted to strengthen the awareness that the message he was bringing came from God. In this he created the space for those in attendance to come to terms with death not only on the basis of the human experience of the finality of our existence, but also on the basis of a biblical-theological eschatological perspective.

---

33. See Masarik, *Analýza nekérygmatických komponentov pohrebných*, 36–42.

God's Word to the bereaved. At the funeral of a young man (age forty-nine) who had gradually weakened and will be missed by his wife, the minister chose the text Isaiah 41:13: "For I, the LORD your God, hold your right hand; it is I who say to you, 'Fear not, I am the one who helps you.'" God demonstrates that he knows about the practical difficulties of the bereaved and the crisis of faith that losing an emotionally important person brings. Both of these facts are covered by a reference to God's goodness. With this choice of text, it is notable that for communicating this reality, the minister found a text where God himself says these words.

God's Word to humans generally. At the funeral of a religiously indifferent elderly gentleman, the minister chose the text Jeremiah 9:23–24a: "Thus says the LORD: 'Let not the wise man boast in his wisdom, let not the mighty man boast in his might, let not the rich man boast in his riches, but let him who boasts boast in this, that he understands and knows me, that I am the LORD who practices steadfast love, justice, and righteousness in the earth.'" Death can call into question many of the successes of a person, but knowing God and his goodness has permanent meaning – for life and for our departure to eternity. As the minister chose this text for the funeral of a religiously indifferent elderly gentleman, the rebuke is impossible not to hear.

ii. The words of the deceased. In the case of a text for a sermon that gives its message in the form of the words of the deceased, there are different categories:

Words of the deceased to their life partner: At the farewell to a good wife and mother whose husband was now left at home alone, the minister chose the text 1 Kings 2:2: "I am about to go the way of all the earth. Be strong, and show yourself a man." They are the words the dying David said to his son Solomon. As in the text, it was a man being addressed, so the minister, even though he shifted the type of relationship (not a parent to son but wife to husband), did not need to make corrections for style. If the minister remained only at the message of the departing to the bereaved, then it would not be a Christian sermon, because in a sermon it is necessary to develop the starting point of faith as the prerequisite so that those left could "be strong."

Words of the deceased to the whole family. At the funeral of a man who had been a key figure in the family and the guardian of family traditions, the minister chose the text Genesis 48:21: "Behold, I am about to die, but God will be with you." By this choice of text, the minister connected to the family which was important for the deceased. This text is excellent to use if the deceased spoke with loved ones about God, and the minister can connect to this fact. If the deceased was religiously indifferent or did not speak for other reasons, then I would regard this choice of text as inappropriate, and for a reference to God's provision, the minister should have chosen another appropriate text.

Words of the deceased to the funeral congregation. At the funeral of the bell ringer whose ringing called the people to church, the minister chose a text which connected to his ministry in the church and which will be the bell ringer's final chime: Isaiah 2:3: "Come, let us go up to the mountain of the LORD, to the house of the God of Jacob, that he may teach us his ways." This choice can be regarded not only as imaginative, but it is also possible to highlight its potential to fulfil the roles of a funeral sermon.

Words of the deceased to God and about God. At the funeral of a devout elderly gentlemen who had been a believer all his life, the minister read Psalm 71:5–6, 9, 14, which is an expression of the testimony of faith of the deceased. The identical relationship between the differentiation and the text for the sermon can be found in the case of a good natured, gentle old man who had a hard life but had been committed to God's will. The text chosen for the sermon was: Psalm 71:5, "For you, O LORD, are my hope, my trust, O LORD, from my youth." This choice of text enabled the deceased to be viewed as a witness to the truthfulness of the biblical message. This limits the use of this approach to cases where the person being buried was unequivocally a Christian.

Words of the deceased about himself. In the case of the tragic death of a young presbyter who was an excellent person, the minister chose as the text Isaiah 38:12: "Like a weaver I have rolled up my life; he cuts me off from the loom." This text excellently captured the situation but it gives less space for textual preaching. It comes across as a groan about a sudden death. I assume that at this kind of funeral, the minister would be praised by those in attendance for such a good choice of text, but I would reconsider this evaluation. This text could form the basis for a general introduction, but the main text of a sermon should enable the minister to speak to the funeral congregation about humans before God.

Words of the deceased to himself. At the funeral of a man in his sixties who through illness had been transformed into a prematurely elderly man, the minister chose the text Psalm 42:5 "Why are you cast down, O my soul, and why are you in turmoil within me? Hope in God; for I shall again praise him." In sermon no. 53, Kiss introduces the fact that it was for the funeral of someone who had suffered. He chose Isaiah 8:17 as the text for the sermon: "I will wait for the LORD, who is hiding his face from the house of Jacob, and I will hope in him." This choice of text indicates a coming to terms with difficulties on the basis of faith in God. Therefore, this choice of text is applicable in cases where the minister can talk about the meaning of faith in difficulties, and this statement convincingly connects to the life style of the deceased.

iii. The words of the bereaved. In this category, Kiss chooses the type of text in which the biblical message is worded in such a way that it is as if the bereaved said it. As examples of this choice we find:

Testimony of the bereaved about the deceased. At the funeral of a much-loved, devout, elderly gentleman, the minister chose the text Luke 2:25: "Now there was a man in Jerusalem, whose name was Simeon, and this man was righteous and devout, waiting for the consolation of Israel."

The biblical text becomes not only the bearer of the message but also a testimony about the deceased.

Testimony of the bereaved about themselves. At the funeral of an older woman who had been a good mother, the minister chose the text Psalm 35:14b: ". . . as one who laments his mother, I bowed down in mourning." The psalmist with these words expresses his participation in the suffering of others. The minister was able to offer the bereaved the chance to express their pain with the psalmist.

Testimony about the certainty of faith. At the funeral of a lonely mother whose young child became an orphan, the minister chose the text Psalm 27:10: "For my father and my mother have forsaken me, but the LORD will take me in." This quote from the Psalms assumes the possibility of the worst scenario, and in the life of this orphan it had happened. She had lost her mother, and she did not have a father. Therefore, the minister through the choice of this text wanted to teach her to have a position of trust in God, like the psalmist, and that she would come to the knowledge of faith and have certainty in God.

The request of the bereaved for spiritual wisdom, forgiveness, and to be led to forgiveness can also become the way to choose the text for the sermon. Under this option, the minister chooses a text whose motivation is a request for spiritual wisdom. Sermon no. 26 was for a funeral for a middle-aged person after a sudden death. Therefore, the minister chose Psalm 90:12 as the text for the sermon: "So teach us to number our days that we may get a heart of wisdom." The ideas in this verse enabled the minister to develop what it means "to get a heart of wisdom." A request for forgiveness, and to be led to forgiveness, was the context of sermon no. 30 for burying a young girl after a suicide. The bereaved were in the situation of coming to terms with feelings of guilt and simultaneously needing to forgive the deceased for the hurt she caused. The choice of one of the requests from the Lord's prayer, ". . . and forgive us our debts, as we also have forgiven our debtors" (Matt 6:12), appears to me to be pastorally legitimate and an appropriate choice for the text of the sermon.

2. When choosing a text for the sermon without considering the differentiation, ministers can choose a text for the sermon based on the church year or the doctrines of the church. The minister can connect to the church year. An example during Advent could be waiting for God in Isaiah 8:17: "I will wait for the LORD, who is hiding his face from the house of Jacob, and I will hope in him." Waiting on God gives suffering a new dimension and brings new strength. Another example could be connecting to the Easter period with the choice of Ezekiel 37:12: "Behold, I will open your graves and raise you from your graves, O my people." The minister here demonstrates that the stimuli from the church year – Easter, with death and resurrection – do not have to be projected into the funeral sermon only as a mechanical overtone of the topic, but it can also be processed from the point of view of the impact on the church.

A choice on the basis of doctrine is for example 2 Timothy 1:10: "Our Saviour Christ Jesus, who abolished death and brought life and immortality to light through the gospel." The minister did not get to this text due to the differentiation or the church year. It was a choice contingent on doctrine, and I regard its use as legitimate.

Each of the aforementioned approaches to choosing a biblical text that will be the basis of the funeral sermon has their strengths and weaknesses. In order to choose the text using different approaches, ministers must first be familiar with them, and on the basis of their own evaluation, judge their benefits and risks. If ministers do this, they will avoid making mistakes that can negatively affect their preaching. Therefore, it is necessary to pay adequate attention to the options for choosing the text for the sermon and apply them in ministry.

Exegesis of the Text of the Sermon

The exegesis of the sermon text is not the only basis for situational homiletics, but it is a supporting discipline. An appropriate use of the biblical text in the funeral sermon depends on good exegesis, which helps the minister to determine the foundational message of the text in its historical context, what is known as "historical-critical exegesis,"[34] and search for the current message for people living today, known as "practical exegesis."[35] The methodological steps for each of these theological disciplines will not be covered here as they are already dealt with extensively in the academic literature.

John Allyn Melloh very aptly points out the problem of the relationship between historical-critical and practical exegesis in the preparation of a funeral sermon. He states that ministers choose their text on the basis of certain pre-critical expectations, and it is from this perspective that they approach the text.[36] As this impacts the later stages, Melloh recommends that once the focus for preaching has been determined, then historical-critical exegesis should only be used as a negative criterion – to make sure no injustice has been done to the text. The positive side of this approach is that ministers are made aware of the necessity of an exegetically defensible approach, but the negative side is that the use of exegesis only to negatively limit the approach means ministers do not actively interact with biblical-theological ideas in the text that could be homiletically processed. Ministers therefore remain reliant on their ability to read the situation and its connection to the chosen text.

Ministers may choose to connect their historical-critical and practical exegesis in whatever way they chose. Yet the one thing that is certain is that they may not arbitrarily assign a meaning to the text that they would like to find there; their starting point must be the meaning that the text actually has.[37]

---

34. A good overview of the basic exegetical approaches can be found in the publication by the Pontifical Biblical Commission, *The Interpretation of the Bible in the Church.*

35. For example, G. D. Fee, *New Testament Exegesis: A Handbook for Students and Pastors* (Louisville: Westminster John Knox, 2002), 195. The risks of the incorrect use of the results of exegesis are demonstrated by J. Kubíková, *Kažte evangelium,* 165: "We cannot rain down theological statements, which we have pulled from the Bible, on the congregation without expressing an understanding of the human experience of joy, expectation or grief."

36. J. A. Melloh states, "Furthermore, to begin homily preparation with historical-critical analysis of the texts – what the texts meant – does not attend sufficiently to the fact that an initial hermeneutical decision was made in selecting the texts. That choice, made pre-critically in keeping with the dynamics of an unarticulated act-scene ratio, is motivated by the here-and-now situation, not by original context or authorial intent." "Homily or Eulogy?," 512.

37. H. Maser states: The interpretation must be exegetically defensible. He does not have to mention everything in the text; his perspective can be specialized and quickly move to emphasizing certain secondary ideas in the text – but he cannot be satisfied with a formal association. Therefore, it is not possible to use the words of Eliezer, "Do not delay me, since the Lord has prospered my way. Send me away that I may go to my master" (Gen 24:56) as the basis of a funeral sermon. Whoever chooses Rev 2:10 must be able to praise more than just marriage and occupational faithfulness! *Die Bestattung* (Gütersloh: Gütersloher Verlagshaus Gerd Mohn, 1964), 49, quoted in Ch. Stebler, *Die drei Dimensionen,* 61.

On the other hand, insufficient and inappropriate exegesis does not allow ministers access to the richness of the Word. Ministers cannot complete their task without it. When the sermon is not based on an exegesis of the biblical text and biblical theology, ministers in the best-case scenario use general religious ideas about death and eternal life. For balance, it must be stated that a loss of a basis in the text does not automatically mean becoming unbiblical. Ministers who are familiar with biblical theology can maintain biblical-theological emphases even when they insufficiently work with a particular biblical text. But if they are not sufficiently familiar with biblical theology, then they can, under the influence of the expectations and ideas of their surroundings, build on ideas that do not come from theologically legitimate sources but from uncritical layers of folk religion.

One of the authors who points out the necessity of the sermon being exegetically anchored is Rudolf Bohren. He states that situational addresses are often a form of injustice to the text of the sermon. He asks whether this is because of poor exegesis or a poor choice of text.[38]

This is a question I also asked when, all over Slovakia at funerals from a variety of church traditions, I inadvertently discovered cases of exegesis being neglected, and frequently the exegesis was indefensible. It is clear that ministers, after the announcement of the funeral, cannot undertake extensive historical-critical exegesis of the chosen text, which is why they should exegete biblical texts that can be used in funeral sermons as part of their ongoing education. When there is not a serious exegetical handling of the text, we are exposed to the following risks:

- The risk of contradicting the function of the text. The use of the biblical text in the funeral sermon frequently reveals poor quality exegetical work, and ministers sometimes do not use the text as the basis for their message but only as an idea that allows them to express situationally conditioned Christian opinions.

---

38. R. Bohren, *Predigtlehre*, 322: "Experience shows that the occasions (weddings and funerals) obviously do not do well to the text. Just marriage and funeral lead the preacher to misuse texts. Also, it might be that the texts themselves are a hindrance to saying what should be said here and now! Or are the texts wrongly chosen?" Similar is Smolík, *Radost ze slova*, 151: "Deforming the funeral sermon into 'religious language' is all the more alarming as it is happening on the basis of a biblical text which in this way is being misused. . . . Based on cases where the biblical text is misused, it follows that the minister must work exegetically with his texts for funeral sermons and that he must clarify his biblical doctrine of death."

- The risk of misusing the biblical text through an interpretation that does not relate to the text.[39]
- The risk of an altered starting point, or basing the funeral sermon on ideas found in "alternative sources." These sources can be different disciplines, for example, art, philosophy, psychology, history, medicine, etc., or a minister's own subjective opinions. The sermon then loses its most important uniqueness – the Word, and "the text essentially has nothing more to say; it merely increases what is said."[40] Ministers can of course use these sources as secondary tools, but they cannot forget that their calling is to preach the Word.
- The risk of altering the essence of the task.
- The risk of a tension between the text and homiletical aims.

Well conducted exegetical work equips ministers to proclaim the Word. It enables them to find the message in the text after clarifying details in the text and their relationships. This exposes ministers to the necessity of making a choice – they must consciously decide which ideas that they have gained from their exegesis they will use, and which they will not, in their funeral sermon. This decision making can be very painful because ministers have obtained these interesting and valuable ideas within tight time constraints. Suddenly they must leave them out of their sermon?

What to leave out? When deciding about what to use and what to leave out, it is helpful for ministers to review their exegetical notes, asking what is necessary to say in the funeral sermon and if it has significance for the bereaved and the wider funeral congregation. This means that ministers must leave out all the interesting ideas from the biblical text that do not relate to the topic of the event and do not fulfil the purpose of a funeral sermon. If ministers do not make this decision, they damage their work from the point of view of (1) content and (2) time.

1. Damage to the content. If ministers are unable to leave out all unnecessary exegetical material, their sermon will be burdened with an abundance of details that do not relate to the homiletical aims or will even prevent them being achieved.

---

39. J. Smolík, *Radost ze slova*, 151. From this he concludes that a necessary part of the work of a minister is exegetical work and the clarification of what the Bible teaches about death.

40. R. Bohren, *Predigtlehre*, 117.

2.   Damage to the timings. A funeral sermon cannot be long. If ministers do not select the most important ideas, they will lose the opportunity to say what is necessary.

Homiletical Meditation

A sermon at a church service brings the message of God's Word to the lives of the listeners. In order for the biblical message to be communicated effectively to contemporary listeners, it is necessary to simultaneously understand the message of the text and to consider the listeners to whom the message is being given. In homiletics it is therefore normal for preparation to consist of three stages: (1) exegesis – understanding the biblical text; (2) homiletical meditation – applied thinking about what this message means for the contemporary listener; and only then follows (3) drafting the sermon – the written formation of the ideas as a whole.

In the phase of homiletical meditation, ministers have already completed their exegesis, and after their meditation will draft the sermon. During their homiletical meditation, ministers ask the questions: "What does this text mean for the listeners that I will address?" Ministers should thus ensure the application of the *kerygma* to the life situation of the listeners. This is a significant task because "inappropriate application can be as destructive as inept exegesis."[41] The experience of ministers shows that this is a task that they can manage well,[42] but it is also possible to fail. Therefore, it is essential that this phase of the homiletical preparation is given proper attention. Vrablec, in this connection and citing Gelineau, draws attention to the following:

- A consideration of the listeners arises from the term "homily," which means an "informal conversation."[43]

---

41. H. Robinson, *Biblical Preaching* (Grand Rapids: Baker, 1980), 28.

42. In practice, we encounter cases where the bereaved state that the Christian funeral ceremony helped them to come to terms with the loss. A widower – and an atheist – approached a minister with the words: "I did not even imagine that a church funeral could help as much. Thank you."

43. J. Gelineau, *L´homélie, forme pléniére de la predication,* in *Maison Dieu,* 82 (Paris: Les editions du Cerf, 1965), no page, quoted in J. Vrablec, *Teologická povaha homílie,* in Vrablec and A. Fabián, *Homiletika I.–II.,* 171. The image presented by Gelineau is the following: "The minister who is preaching the homily is above all else a friend who is speaking to a friend who he knows and loves in order to help him, enlighten him, strengthen him and "construct" the words of salvation. He adapts to the listeners, their needs and abilities, their language and culture, their human and Christian surroundings. The homily is an expression of care in the spirit of a

- A consideration of the listeners should form one of two centre points of the sermon, which should be understood as an oval with two centre points: the text and the listeners.[44]

In one sense, these two centre points of the sermon can be encountered in the study by Michalko of sermon styles.[45] In one of his monitored periods, he observed how ministers establish the topic and how they elaborate on it. Michalko demonstrates that the sermon can be based on practical observations and the message is then processed biblically (known as the practical-biblical style), or the sermon can be based on exegesis of the text and the message inferred to real-life conditions (known as the biblical-practical style). Both of these styles take the listeners into consideration, and in my opinion, they both have their own value, advantages, and disadvantages. In both it is significant that they result in a sermon which has a defined problem which is resolved from the perspective of the Scriptures, while considering the processes of the listeners.

If the sermons that I observed were to be categorized on the basis of the criteria of establishing the topic and resolving the problem in the church service sermon, we would have to create more groups that should never occur: (a) a practical-practical style and (b) a biblical-biblical style.

a. A practical-practical style occurs when ministers discern the practical questions and problems that the believers have. Yet the resolutions they provide in the sermon are not from the biblical text but from "practical" observations, experiences, and opinions without any connection to the text of the sermon and its biblical context.[46] The text of the sermon is formally connected to the address, but in terms of meaning it is subordinate, acting merely as a backdrop

---

shepherd who knows and loves God's Word and knows and loves his people, and therefore is in a virtual dialogue with them through his informal conversation."

44. J. Vrablec, "Tematické a cyklické kázne," in Vrablec and Fabián, *Homiletika I.–II.*, 189, references Kamphaus's research on the primary relationship of the text to the listener in the sermon. They point out various possibilities for the position that the listeners can have in the minister's approach and lists the consequences that arise from these shifts. If the text is in the centre, it can lead to a weakening of the position of the listeners. If the listeners are in the centre, it weakens the position of the biblical text.

45. J. Michalko, *Kázňové smery.*

46. Bohren, *Predigtlehre*, 322, asks about the relationship between the biblical text and the funeral, if the text interprets the events or only decorates it. He asks something similar on page 117 – whether the text discusses the topic of the funeral sermon or if it is only some kind of "background music" to it.

to the words of the minister. Despite the fact that this approach can strike a chord with the listeners, it must, from a theological perspective, be regarded as unacceptable, because it renounces its principal role – proclaiming the Word. This function is replaced by material from secondary sources.

b.   A biblical-biblical style has its starting point in the text of the Bible, and as well as starting there it also finishes there. The listeners are not shown the impact of God's Word for their current lives. As the practical-practical approach was rejected for losing the Word, the biblical-biblical approach must be criticized for its incomplete message, as it does not move to the kerygmatic and catechetical consequences of the text for the listeners today. Though formally it is faithful to the biblical text, according to Vrablec and Fabián, this type of approach without considering the listeners is a form of unfaithfulness to the biblical text because "the Bible considers the listener to be a partner. And we are from this positon removing them to the situation of being merely props or a backdrop."[47] This kind of approach to preaching weakens the relationship of the listeners to the biblical text because it supports the notion that the minister brought interesting and nice ideas that are not applicable to real life.

During my observations at funerals, I repeatedly encountered the problem of an inadequate connection between the biblical message and the homiletical situation of the listeners. This problem can be described by two experiences.

As a part of a workshop on homiletics, along with my students of theology, I attended a number of funerals. At one of them a young minister gave an excellent evangelistic sermon. But because he forgot that the people in front of him were sitting next to the coffin of their mother, I had to evaluate his sermon as being an excellent evangelistic sermon but a terrible funeral sermon.

This evaluation was confirmed to me a couple of years later. During field observations at a funeral ceremony of a young man in 2008, I met his uncle who was my friend. He is not a member of any Christian church. The minister gave a high quality and clearly Christocentric testimony, but he did not connect it to the situation of the grieving family, and contemporary man as he is. After the ceremony, I asked my friend if the funeral sermon had interested him. He and his wife answered that "The minister had to say his stuff, but we would

47. J. Vrablec and A. Fabián, *Homiletika I.–II.*, 190.

have preferred it if he had said more about our Mickey."[48] To my clarifying question about whether the sermon gave them anything, they replied that they are not religious types and that part of the ceremony had not interested them.

I regarded it as a pity that the sermon remained on the level of biblical-theological pronouncements. The minister did not search for the significance of his content for his listeners, so he enabled them to ignore the biblical message. He maintained the cultural and aesthetical value of the ceremony but missed the opportunity for it to be a true help for handling loss or a help for those searching for orientation in life or needing it be strengthened.

Homiletical meditations should show the listeners that the minister "is not just saying his stuff, what he had to say," but is paying attention to them on the basis of the biblical text. Ministers are here for them, and by using God's Word, ministers comfort and admonish them. What ministers say should not come across as some imaginary religious concepts but should relate to that particular funeral congregation, the deceased, the bereaved, and themselves.

Methodological notes

The need to "know" the listeners. Ministers need to think about the text for the sermon in a virtual dialogue with the listeners, connecting to their certainties and uncertainties, doubts and searching. If ministers can connect the listeners' situation to the text for the sermon, those attending the funeral will feel that they are not just a backdrop, but that they have met with the minister as they search for answers to their serious existential and spiritual questions. When these questions are answered on the basis of the Bible, they receive the comfort faith brings.

Haddon Robinson states that "The expositor must know his people as well as his message. . . . Expository sermons today will be ineffective unless the preacher realizes that his listeners too exist at a particular address and have mindsets unique to them."[49] This statement sounds too difficult, realizing that the minister cannot actually know the listeners of the funeral sermon as many of them will have travelled a long distance to be there, and the minister will not have met them before. However, ministers can focus on the problems and thinking of people today. Bill Hybels develops this idea that to know the listeners means to know intimately, "how the minds of his listeners' work,"[50]

---

48. The name has been changed.

49. H. Robinson, *Biblical Preaching*, 27.

50. B. Hybels, "Speaking to the Secularized Mind," in B. Hybels, H. Robinson, and S. Briscoe, *Mastering Contemporary Preaching* (Portland: Multnomah, 1989).

or understand how they really think and their values. Ministers must learn to communicate with people, as they are, and the ideas in the sermon should reflect this knowledge. For us it means a need to know how our listeners subjectively decide whether the proclaimed gospel is acceptable or not, their objections to the text of the sermon, and possible doubts about the faith.[51] On each of these aspects, ministers cannot just operate verbally, because responding to the message is not just a question of reason.

The German evangelical theologian, Adolf Pohl, advised his students that while they are preparing their sermons, they should have in mind several typical people from their church who they know and whose questions and objections to the ideas in the sermon they can predict.[52] This helps to promote a virtual dialogue with these listeners and through them to the others who will attend. This helps the sermon to be generally understandable and acceptable for the listeners.

The minister's perceptiveness and ability to predict the problems which listeners are dealing with limits this kind of virtual dialogue. Ministers must remember that people grieving deeply sometimes lose their faith in God. Others keep their faith but may experience disappointment. Therefore, ministers must attempt to find comforting words which are not a denial of reality but enable the listeners to cope with God's help.

The necessity for truthful and pastorally sensitive thinking. Ministers must present their biblical-theological emphases truthfully and in a pastorally sensitive way. Here the term "truthful" is understood as meaning the ministers' interpretation of the particular situation from the perspective of the theology of their church. Despite the differences in how people interpret soteriological questions, ministers cannot scare them with judgement, the accountability of people to God, or speak about Christ's grace as if the gospel did not require people to make a decision to live a life of faith. Pastoral sensitivity should be understood as a presentation that people are accountable to God, but in which the listeners are invited to obtain faith or to deepen their faith and that does not create a manipulative pressure which has negative impacts.

Ecumenical sensitivity as a part of pastoral sensitivity. A Christian funeral is a place for administering comfort and reassessing attitudes to life – from the perspective of our human standing before God and the awareness of our

---

51. Similar is J. Vrablec and A. Fabián, *Homiletika I.–II.*, 298: "Another prerequisite is an in-depth knowledge of your listeners, their objections, hindrances and difficulties with the faith."

52. I was taught by Adolf Pohl at the Freier Evangelischer Gemeinden seminary in the German Democratic Republic during the school year of 1983/84.

mortality. Therefore, it is not an appropriate place for ministers to insensitively stress particular emphases of their church in contrast to the doctrines of other churches. The following reasons can be given for being ecumenically sensitive:

a. Ecumenical responsibility. A funeral ceremony is usually conducted by a minister from one church, but the bereaved and the funeral congregation can be members of different churches. The minister must therefore accept the task of becoming "their minister," meaning accepting the ecumenical responsibility to perform spiritual ministry for all those in attendance. This is why during a homiletical meditation, ministers must focus on essential facts.

b. Pastoral purpose. Respect towards the deceased and empathy with the grieving helps ministers to remove from the sermon everything that could needlessly cause conflict. Ministers do not take this approach because they are uncertain about what they believe but out of respect for the bereaved, who are burdened with grief and should be able to expect that ministers will bring peace and spiritual support. Therefore, ministers should not add to their burden by opening up doctrinal disputes.[53] The funeral ceremony is also not the right place for an "exhibition" of ministers' exegetical work. Ministers are not there in order to confirm their abilities but to serve people at a time of crisis.

Searching for meaning. An analysis of the sermon applications given by ministers reveals the pastoral wisdom of some. But for other ministers, it is merely an exercise in formally connecting some ideas from a sense of duty and not as a result of their genuine struggle to apply God's Word to the situation of the funeral congregation. Inadequate development of the application of the message is, based on my observations, often combined with additional persuasive pressure on the listeners. It would be more appropriate if ministers offered them the message of the sermon by developing their trust in God and demonstrating the reliability, legitimacy, and functionality of the message.

If ministers do not always think afresh about the application of the message and instead rely on what they usually say, then they harm both the listeners and

---

53. This comment should not limit ministers when preaching on biblical teaching that is in accordance with the doctrines of their church. After all, the family of the deceased expressed their agreement when they requested them to conduct the ceremony. Emphases that distinguish a minister's church from others should be presented unequivocally but with humility and the attitude of being a witness so that those in attendance will be invited to think about them, and ministers should never be disparaging about other approaches.

themselves.[54] The listeners are harmed because ministers do not bring them a relevant message, and ministers harm themselves as they prevent their own development as ministers.

Stylizing the Sermon

A funeral sermon is constructed from two main source areas: the biblical message and the contact with the case.[55] Ministers have chosen the text and completed its exegesis. They have meditated about what the message means for those they expect or assume will be at the funeral. Now they must formulate this material in a written form.

A funeral sermon, and for that matter all sermons, are not written in "one breath." Of course, the first draft can be written in one sitting, which I recommend. But then it is advisable to leave the writing and do something completely different, so that the thought patterns behind the formulation of the written sermon are no longer there. Looking again at the draft after some time, even a short time, can help to perceive its shortcomings. It should not be forgotten that it is an address for the difficult moment of saying farewell. It therefore merits an appropriate degree of dignity and pastoral sensitivity, which must be reflected in the wording of the funeral sermon.

Forms of Expression

Pastoral ministry in crisis situations requires appropriate forms of expression. Sometimes an appropriate form of expression is remaining silent; at other times, it is to use words.[56] Naturally, the message that ministers convey in the

---

54. C. Hürlimann characterizes pastorally effective communication as listening and offering "helpful words." He characterizes this type of word as follows: "It will not be a rash word, not a word that overflows the mourner. It will not be a word that demands. Most likely a word that invites. Perhaps we can speak about our own experience. Whether our partner can learn from it? Perhaps we are talking about an experience that others have done. In this context belong the experiences of faith, as the Bible tells us. The Bible contains many and very varied reports of people who have experienced God's closeness in a difficult time. There are many possibilities, then, to express our confidence in our words, that during difficult times we do not depend on ourselves, but we are held fast by God." *Ich will mit dir gehen*, 8.

55. Also H. H. Jenssen, *Die kirchliche Handlungen*, 179: "In regard to preaching at funerals, it is possible to distinguish between general, foundational and special moments, which touched the deceased and their life."

56. P. Sheppy states, "Those who minister to the dying and the bereaved must be willing to be silent where words would be empty. At the same time, we have to say something – and we have something to say." *Death Liturgy and Ritual*, vol. 1, 108.

funeral sermon should not be merely the communication of empty phrases. They bring it from a source which they find in God, and their word, and take it to people in a particular homiletical situation.

But even when ministers have appropriate content, it is not certain that its communication will occur without any hindrance. Communication theory talks about the formulating (encoding) by the speaker and understanding (decoding) of a message by the audience. If ministers "encode" their message in such a way that the listeners cannot "decode" it, if they do not understand the words and concepts, it reduces the effectiveness of the transfer of the biblical message. In this connection, it is essential to especially have in mind the unchurched people attending the funeral. As an expression of consideration to them, ministers should consider the content, the treatment of the topic, and stylization. Religious terms are known to active Christians, but without explanation they are a meaningless code for the unchurched and useless words even though ministers intend them to be bearers of meaning.[57]

Cultural and Theological Adequacy: Language Level of Speech

Ministers must stylize their sermon in such a way that it is understood by Christians and contemporary people who do take part in church life. Keeping the expressions up to date is a constant task of theology. If this search for culturally suitable means of expression is not managed, it can lead to alienation from the topic or the alienation of the listeners.

The risk of expressions alienating the topic

Unmanaged cultural adaption of forms of expression betrays inadequate biblical-theological work and inadequate biblical evaluation of the phenomenon being thought about. According to the seriousness it can be labelled as (1) underestimating the theological phenomenon or (2) loss of theological anchoring.

1. Underestimating the theological phenomenon. Stebler points out the risk of inappropriately chosen words when after quoting a passage from an analyzed sermon, he states, "The life of a person as 'a picture' of God is a good picture which bestows man great honour. But the

---

57. In the gospels there are several situations where, because the expression had more than one meaning, it caused the content to be misunderstood. One example is John 11:13 where John states, "Now Jesus had spoken of his death, but they thought that he meant taking rest in sleep." Similarly, Paul in 1 Thess 5:10, "Who died for us so that whether we are awake or asleep we might live with him," prompts the reader to ask the question what he should understand by the word "asleep."

classification of sin as 'a hardening' and 'a darkening' leads to the underestimation of sin."[58]

2. Loss of theological anchoring. In this case, ministers use theological terms, but conceptually they are so far removed from the Bible that their theological ideas become detached from any biblical context. This is demonstrated by statements in a sermon that diminish the power of death by labelling it "a messenger of God" or "the angel of death," which ministers are unable to exegetically justify.[59]

When analyzing sermons, I noticed that ministers use some terms that have multiple meanings in independent fields. An example is a sermon where the minister first talked about "the death of the body" in the biological meaning, yet later in his sermon used the phrase "they live on." He shifted from a biological to a theological-eschatological meaning.

This opens up the question of how ministers should use theological expressions which also have a non-religious meaning. How can ministers work with them in such a way that the listeners are always clear which meaning of the expression is being used? Is it necessary to refer to any shifts in the meaning? Can ministers use words with the meaning found in colloquial speech? Should they reserve these words only for use with biblical content? The problem is that if ministers reserve these words only for theological content, then non-religious people attending the funeral will understand them to have their normal colloquial meaning. However ministers approach this question, it is important to avoid misleading overlapping meanings as well as expressions that are complicated or that prevent the sermon from being understandable.

The risk of expressions alienating the listeners

It can be observed that ministers who are fresh out of seminary have a problem with their use of language alienating their listeners as they have not learned to transfer their ideas from a university setting to normal life.[60] There are also forms of expression used by older ministers with more experience that lack clarity, which also means an inadequate evangelistic sensitivity. They address

---

58. Ch. Stebler, *Die drei Dimensionen*, 36.

59. Ibid., 43.

60. P. Sheppy, *Death Liturgy and Ritual, vol. 1*, 18: "There is nothing new in this, but it does serve to illustrate the gulf between the language of theological discourse and popular belief. In the funeral, when the Christian Church seeks to minister to the bereaved, this gulf can quickly become a credibility gap."

their listeners technically very well, but form their ideas as if their audience only consisted of active, well-taught Christians.

Structure and Length of the Funeral Sermon

This section first focuses on the structure and then on the length of a funeral sermon.

The Structure of a Funeral Sermon

The disciples on the road to Emmaus and the structure of a funeral sermon

The gospel description of the disciples on the road to Emmaus (Luke 24:13–35) is one of the New Testament texts that is closest to the subject of funeral sermons.[61] These disciples are people who are disappointed because of the loss of a close friend whom they had expected to make a significant difference to their lives – and there is a proclaimed word. These factors mean the account has a paradigmatic significance for resolving theological questions about funeral sermons. The question can be asked, "Why does Jesus express an interest in the topic of their conversation (v. 17)[62] when he could have immediately expressed the joy of the resurrection?" I believe that his approach was designed to create space for an authentic dialogue in which those addressed will be able to personally come to terms at the end with the message of his resurrection (v. 32).[63]

The whole structure of the narrative focuses not only on Jesus's approach but also on the fact that his approach leads the originally grieving disciples to a gradual coming to terms with the good news.

Possibility to connect. For today's funeral sermons, this account illustrates the need for openness to the articulation of pain and disappointment in such a way that in the end, these statements become a part of the proclamation of the gospel when they are reappraised after "the story is completed" with reference to God's actions with humans through the resurrection and eternal life. This "completing" has the potential to provide a significant source of comfort

---

61. About the use of this pericope for general homiletical questions, see J. Vrablec and A. Fabián, *Homiletika I.–II.*, 24.

62. Luke 24:17: "And he said to them, 'What is this conversation that you are holding with each other as you walk?' And they stood still, looking sad."

63. Luke 24:32: "They said to each other, 'Did not our hearts burn within us while he talked to us on the road, while he opened to us the Scriptures?'"

and hope as the biblical message is not brought as a foreign element but as a perspective on what has just been experienced – from the perspective of faith.

Perceiving the loss as prerequisite for kerygmatic completion. On this basis, I believe that a funeral sermon can only refer to the eschatological perspective comprehensibly and truthfully when it is open to perceiving the loss from our earthly perspective. Without this prerequisite, the hope of the resurrection can be turned into a shallow attempt at escaping from an unbearable reality. This can occur because of insufficiencies on two levels – theological and pastoral. On both of these levels, it is reducing the size of the Christian hope in the resurrection. Therefore, it is important that the structure of the sermon creates factual prerequisites so the *kerygma* is not relativized but that the listeners would be enabled to receive it.

Situational preaching practice and the structure of the address

As with all forms of oral speech, it is also true of funeral sermons that they have an introduction, body, and conclusion. Although it may seem that arrangement of the address is above all a matter of rhetoric and stylization, the structure of a funeral sermon must be theologically constructed, and each part needs to be theologically justified. Therefore, the structure should also be regarded as a theological dimension. From the Slovak context, the following impetuses can be found.

Vrablec takes as his starting point the four foundational functions[64] *kerygma, didaskalia, paraklesis,* and *mystagogia,* which when understood "create the prerequisites for a correct homiletical construction."[65] Therefore in the whole of one extensive chapter on homiletics (ch. 6), he elaborates these four functions as four parts of a homily, to which at the end he adds "an introduction" (6.5) and "a conclusion" (6.6). This approach can definitely be regarded as theologically justified, and therefore without doubt it is also usable in Protestant situational-homiletical work. A detailed description of the structure of funeral sermons in the Lutheran church can be found in the introduction to the theoretical treatise in Igor Kišš's collection of his funeral sermons. It consists of the following parts:

---

64. J. Vrablec and A. Fabián, *Homiletika I.–II.,* 72, in the "sense of biblical theological doctrines and official church teaching after the Second Vatican Council." For *kerygma* as a part of the homiletical structure, see 112–120. For *didaskalia* as a part of the homiletical structure, see 121–128. For *paraklesis* as a part of the homiletical structure, see 128–132. For *mystagogia* as a part of the homiletical structure, see 132–142.

65. Ibid., 112.

1. A general introduction.
2. Addressing the bereaved.
3. A bridge to the biblical text.
4. The biblical text and work with it. This part could be understood as a funeral sermon in the narrow sense of the word. It has three sections, and the final one has an eschatological emphasis.
5. Conclusion and departing in the hope of the resurrection.

A more detailed description of this structure can be found in Kišš's text[66] as well as in my analysis of his funeral sermons.[67]

Further information about the structure of funeral sermons can be obtained by personally analyzing funeral sermons. When I have asked ministers about the structure of their funeral sermons, they answered that the individual parts they develop intuitively, even though when listening or reading the sermon, it can be found that they work on the basis of some kind of framework that helps them achieve effective results.

For ministers who would feel too constrained if they had to consciously take into consideration a situational-homiletical model, I recommend that they at least check to see if their approach is in accordance with the three dimensions of funeral sermons that are emphasized by Stebler – (1) the theology,[68] (2) the deceased,[69] and (3) the funeral congregation[70] – and that these three dimensions are arranged appropriately for the case and the text for the sermon.

Even though the idea of not working with a homiletical structure may offer ministers the feeling that they have greater freedom, I suspect that this kind of "freedom" is more of a burden than a benefit. This is because ministers must make decisions when they are pressed for time without something to refer to. Therefore, I regard it as being very important that ministers create funeral sermons using a clear homiletical approach. This only appears to make redundant internal expectations of God's guidance during preparation. A structure can aid ministers to ask questions, and these they can answer after

---

66. I. Kišš, *Nádej nad hrobom*, 1, 3.
67. A. Masarik, *Analýza nekérygmatických komponentov pohrebných*. The whole of this monograph is devoted to a detailed study of the individual parts.
68. Ch. Stebler, *Die drei Dimensionen*, 65–80.
69. Ibid., 81–116.
70. Ibid., 117–130.

reflecting on the case and the message in prayer. This ensures that during their preparation, ministers do not overlook any important parts of their task.

What I also regard as beneficial when preaching a funeral sermon are the following: trust in the proclaimed Word and its impact on the bereaved,[71] and focusing on one comforting truth from the biblical text and its pastoral use in the homiletical framework.[72]

The Length of a Funeral Sermon

Jiřina Kubíková presents conflicting information about the appropriate length of a situational address. On the one hand, she states that, "Due to the celebratory and ceremonial character of this church occasion, the sermon can be richer and longer,"[73] but in the section which only relates to funeral sermons, she says, "the message must be always short, factual, and directed to strike the heart of the listener."[74] In the wider ecumenical discussion of this question, there is a consensus that excessively long sermons are generally damaging. The Agenda of the Evangelical Church of Czech Brethren advises that "sermons and prayers should not be long."[75] Sugden and Wiersbe believe that "long services often deepen the wounds,"[76] and an inappropriately long sermon combined with "heartlessness" is even regarded by Axman and Aleš as "cruelty."[77] Judith Wray also states that, "The needs of the mourners will probably be better served by a short and simple sermon that does not oversimplify the gospel message of life in the face of death."[78] Bryan Chapell argues for a short funeral sermon

71. B. Chapell states: "*Simple truths sincerely spoken are required.* This is not the time for theological treatises or exegetical insights. The simple truths of our resurrection and reunion based upon God's grace alone are the most compelling, meaningful, and comforting things you can say. The gospel has real power in these moments. Do not be afraid to let the Word do its work." *Christ-Centered Preaching*, 344.

72. H. F. Sugden and W. W. Wiersbe state, "Your message should focus on one comforting truth; this is no time for a doctrinal exegesis on death or resurrection. You are applying balm to broken hearts, so be tender." *Confident Pastoral Leadership*, 104. Also, Chapell says, "Messages typically are a logical development of a basic idea (or two) in a text, not verse-by-verse expositions – no one will have their Bibles with them to follow along." *Christ-Centered Preaching*, 344.

73. J. Kubíková, *Kažte evangelium*, 165.

74. Ibid.,166.

75. *Agenda ČCE* (Agenda of the Evangelical Church of Czech Brethren [ECCB], 1983), 195.

76. H. F. Sugden and W. W. Wiersbe, *Confident Pastoral Leadership*, 104.

77. P. O. Axman and P. Aleš, *Homiletika*, 83.

78. J. H. Wray, "Preaching Life in the Face of Death," 40.

from the fact that it is a very difficult time for the bereaved.[79] In his opinion, a sermon longer that five to ten minutes indicates a lack of sensitivity from the minister. As an exception, he quotes the case where the family requested a longer more traditional sermon. Chapell also regards as an exception cases when the "stature of the deceased and/or particularly tragic circumstances may also require a more lengthy address."[80]

The length of the sermon can be determined (1) as an expression of time (in minutes) or (2) by the number of words.

1. Length of the funeral sermon expressed in minutes. The usual length of a funeral sermon is probably six to ten minutes, and this length varies not only between different church traditions but also in each tradition. In later research, it would be beneficial to precisely monitor the usual length of the sermon and what is an acceptable deviation from this length in each church tradition. Deviations from this framework during the period when I carried out my field observations at the crematorium in Banská Bystrica, Slovakia, were the following:

    a. The shortest sermon lasted two and a half minutes. The number in its own may sound incredibly short, but as a part of the liturgy of the Catholic funeral rite, such a short address did not create any subjective negative feelings in those attending. The question though remains whether in such a short time the address could achieve its purposes.

    b. The longest sermon lasted forty-one minutes. The Lutheran minister ensured he had the time for such an extensive address by making sure the funeral was the last one for that particular day – which removed the risk that it would overrun into the time assigned to the following funeral ceremony. As a theologian, I followed the sermon with interest, but I noticed that a number of those in attendance had stopped listening, and because out of courtesy they could not leave, they had begun to stare at the ceiling.

    The time available for the sermon depends on the total time the minister has for conducting the ceremony at the burial site and the extent of the prescribed liturgy. Therefore, it is easy for anyone

---

79. B. Chapell, *Christ-Centered Preaching*, 344.
80. Ibid.

to determine the time framework they have based on their church tradition: total length of the ceremony minus the time required for liturgical actions equals the time available for the funeral sermon. The overall length of the ceremony at the crematorium is on average approximately twenty-five minutes: the time before the body goes for cremation or is buried in the ground.[81] In villages, there is often less time pressure, but the minister should take care not to abuse this fact.

2. Length of the sermon by the number of words. Six hundred to nine hundred, in some cases up to eleven thousand words, can be regarded as the usual length of funeral sermons in many Christian churches.[82] Sermons significantly longer or shorter than this range were rarely observed. An indicative value for the most common length is approximately nine hundred words.

Non-Kerygmatic and Kerygmatic Components of Funeral Sermons

After a detailed analysis of funeral sermons, I discovered that they contain components that can be labelled as "non-kerygmatic," those that for good reasons are included in the funeral sermon but do not contain the biblical message, and components that can be labelled "kerygmatic," those that contain the biblical message of faith.[83]

---

81. K. Willhite suggests that most funerals should not exceed twenty minutes. In the cultural context of Slovakia, this can apply for funerals at the crematorium. When the body is being buried into the ground, the ceremony is lengthened by the movement of the funeral congregation from the chapel to the place the coffin will be buried and the liturgical acts at the graveside. "Title of Article," in *Contemporary Handbook*, eds. A. Malphurs and K. Willhite, 151.

82. These values I obtained by measuring the length of funeral sermons that I received as Word documents from a variety of ministers. This observation does not reflect the differentiation between the different church traditions.

83. These parts of the funeral sermon are being labelled as kerygmatic based on the Greek New Testament term "kerygma" (*kērygma*), which according to J. B. Souček, means "(1) announcement declared by an announcer, proclamation; (2) In the New Testament ordinarily, message (declared by God's announcer and its contents is the redeeming acts of God) preaching." *Řecko-český slovník k Novému zákonu* (Praha: KEBF, 1973), 143. This term is in the academic discourse used to denote the content of the early Christian message. In its early form, it is found expressed in the formula "kyrios Christos," which expressed that Jesus of Nazareth was the promised Messiah. The gospels give a message about his teaching, wonders, and finally his death and resurrection as a testimony which should lead to and strengthen faith in him. Paul demonstrates that his message (*kērygma*) is fully dependent on Christ's resurrection (1 Cor 15:14: "And if Christ has not been raised, then our preaching (*kērygma*) is in vain and your faith is in vain.").

Non-Kerygmatic Components – Case and Context

I have covered the question of the non-kerygmatic component of funeral sermons in a separate monograph.[84] Examples of this component are culturally appropriate methods of establishing contact and details about the deceased that are not used in relation to the biblical text. Even though these parts of the funeral sermon do not communicate the biblical message, they are, if the minister has the correct attitude, a prerequisite for empowering the kerygmatic and pastoral dimensions of the funeral sermon. By leaving them out, ministers "gain" more time for the kerygmatic part, but this would be at the risk that the sermon would sound like a collection of religious opinions without any link to the listeners' difficult situation. Therefore, it definitely is not a loss, in fact it is beneficial if ministers connect to the situation of those in attendance and the life of the deceased and in an appropriate way then move to the biblical message.

Kerygmatic Components – The Biblical Message

A funeral sermon communicates God's Word and through this contributes to the process of change. It is not only a description of the existing state, death and grieving, but it also shows the relevance to all in attendance of God's work in Christ: what God did and changed for the deceased, for the bereaved, and for the rest of the grieving congregation. In this way, the sermon either directly or indirectly shows the potential to come to terms with the loss, a process that the bereaved have now begun.

It can be said that the Bible sets the boundaries for the scope of the kerygmatic component. When preaching at a funeral, ministers need to ask, "What is the relationship between the New Testament *kerygma* and the homiletical situation of funerals in general?" Simultaneously, ministers need to consider how the specifics of the funeral of a particular deceased person should influence the *kerygma*. After analyzing funeral sermons, it is possible to observe that these requirements are often not fulfilled.

The funeral says that death occurred. Therefore, it is necessary to search for the New Testament understanding and meaning of death. Ministers also need to ask about the biblical message that they should share with people who are coming to terms with the death of a loved one.

After a loss, people grieve. Therefore, it is necessary for ministers to search for a New Testament approach to grieving, including its acceptance and support

---

84. A. Masarik, *Analýza nekérygmatických komponentov pohrebných.*

to process it. But it also opens a further set of questions, such as the state of the deceased and those attending the funeral service. Ministers should not simply express empathy and share a testimony about trusting God. This content is very valuable and must be part of the context of a minister's work, but the role of the minister is to proclaim God's Word.

The content, New Testament kerygmatic emphases, is a subject of New Testament theology. For practical reasons, it is necessary to show the need to elaborate individual topics of funeral sermons from the relevant fields of theological investigation in such a way that it can be summarized in a form that will be usable for situational homiletics in order to give dynamism to the proclamation at funerals.

Details about the Deceased Person

In connection with the aspects of a funeral sermon, it was stated that the personality of the deceased must be reflected in the construction of the funeral. It would be possible to formally comply with this requirement by combining any "evangelistic" sermon and the details of the case.[85] But handling a funeral in this way cannot be regarded as being satisfactory. Therefore, there should be an effort to appropriately use the stimuli that are provided by the case, and with both pastoral and preaching sensitivity, take them into consideration in the sermon. This role is the most easily completed when the deceased was unequivocally a Christian.

Stebler claims that "In our age a biographical portrayal and an individualized funeral sermon appears to be essential."[86] On this basis he states that "it is not a question of whether but how to arrange the biography and preaching in the funeral sermon."[87]

In chapter 1 in the section, "Other Addresses at Funerals," it was said there are two foundational approaches alongside each other – "a sermon" and "a eulogy." Their foundational concepts differ in that a funeral sermon has God and his Word as its focal point. It provides a testimony about God's work in Christ and the offers and demands on our lives that emerge from that work. From this starting point, the funeral sermon gives a biblical message to the

---

85. Here the details of the case are understood to mean at a Protestant funeral ceremony, information about the life of the deceased and details about the individuals or family who are saying farewell to the deceased.

86. Ch. Stebler, *Die drei Dimensionen*, 41.

87. Ibid., 42.

situation of loss, the theocentric approach. Therefore, statements about the deceased cannot be the focal point of a funeral sermon. Kubíková warns that a minister must avoid two extreme positions: one is placing the deceased at the centre of the message, and the other is to not pay any attention at all to the person.

1) The deceased is the focal point of the proceedings. The funeral is then only based on ideas arising from the personality of the deceased and that person's impact on the life of the family and on society. This approach achieves a high degree of personalization of the proceedings, but at the cost of losing a Christian sermon. This, therefore, means that the tools for supporting the completion of the other roles of a funeral are missing.

2) The deceased is not paid attention to at all, because the celebrant understands the address as an occasional address that has its focal point away from the case of the deceased. In this kind of case, even if the funeral sounded dignified, it is missing a prerequisite for fulfilling one of its main roles – a farewell to the deceased.[88]

A eulogy in contrast desires to pay respect to the life of the deceased, an anthropocentric approach, even though this aim is sometimes realized using religious language.

We must keep in mind these differing aims when talking about any questions connected to references to the deceased person in the funeral sermon. This means that a Christian funeral address should be a sermon which is theologically constructed. The deceased, the grieving, and the whole congregation should be placed before God, and his Word should be brought to the situation of saying farewell and loss. If this role was given up, it would be a loss in a number of ways. This is why it is possible to understand the Roman Catholic approach which minimizes the space for talking about the deceased person as an attempt to keep a biblical emphasis and as a protection against the mistakes that occur when proclaiming the Word is replaced by praising the person. However, this does not mean that the mistake of putting too much emphasis on the deceased cannot be avoided and a way found to process this stimulus in a theologically legitimate way.

---

88. J. Kubíková, *Kažte evangelium*, 165.

Reasons for Using Details about the Deceased

Discourses about theological reasons that support the inclusion of details about the deceased person into the funeral sermon include the following ideas: an incarnational understanding of the Word; human life as God's gift; the reliability of the biblical message; and the responsibility of humans to God.

An incarnational understanding of the Word

Smolík states that exclusion of the deceased from the funeral sermon conflicts with an incarnational understanding of the Word.[89] He points to the incarnation of Christ and its impact on human existence. On this basis, it is possible to conclude that overlooking the deceased due to a focus on the message is not "a theologically better approach" but a retreat from an area in which the Word should manifest itself in human existence.

Human life as a gift from God

Out of respect for human life as a gift from God, it is not possible to exclude remembrance of the deceased from the funeral sermon. This can mean in certain circumstances that gratitude is expressed to God for the good which was received by the bereaved and the wider community through the life of the deceased.

The inclusion of details about the deceased demonstrates both respect to the life of the deceased person and a responsiveness to the expectations of the bereaved and the wider funeral congregation. Originally, I had intended to classify these reasons as "non-theological," but because of Jesus's double commandment to love both God and our neighbour (Matt 22:34–40), these reasons also gain a theological dimension. Ministers express love to God through responsible proclamation of his Word. Love to humans is expressed through what ministers pay attention to:[90]

- The case of the deceased, by the fact that ministers do not conduct the funeral impersonally, without any interest in the person who has died. But on the contrary, by paying attention to the deceased,

---

89. J. Smolík, *Radost ze slova*, 151.

90. H. H. Jenssen understands the mentioning of details from the life of the deceased *sub specie aeternitatis* as an expression of Christian love towards the deceased and the bereaved. *Die kirchliche Handlungen*, 183. J. Jamnický comes to the same conclusion but from the point of view of an absence of a consideration of the deceased, "a mere objective message from the Word of God could be regarded in certain cases as showing a lack of love and compassion." *Evanjelické pohrebné kázne*, 79.

ministers enter into the deceased's social network so that in that context, ministers are able to fulfil their kerygmatic task.

- The case of the bereaved and the funeral congregation, by supporting their expectations and need to say farewell to the deceased. Sheppy and Carr observe very clearly that those requesting a funeral often do not expect the proclamation of the Word but want "to use" the church ceremony to express their feelings and needs.[91] This observation opens various critical questions about the meaning and legitimacy of proceedings which are being "used." Despite this, I hold the opinion that ministers should proclaim the Word in instances when they are requested to minister on the basis of expectations that they would critically appraise. Their approach to their ministry can help to correct these expectations and simultaneously fulfil expectations that are not in contradiction with faith. Naturally, I feel strongly that ministers must view their role as that of preaching the gospel. But this does not automatically mean that the funeral should not fulfil theologically legitimate needs of the bereaved and the funeral congregation.

The reliability of the biblical message

Jenssen's approach is similar to Smolík's, but he places a greater emphasis on attention spans. According to him, the Christian witness about God stooping down to humans becomes unbelievable if there is insufficient remembrance of the deceased in the funeral sermon.[92] He goes on to state that ministers who want to preach effectively that our great God regards impoverished human souls as valuable must themselves demonstrate that they think that way. Therefore, it will, in Jenssen's opinion, nearly always give the wrong impression if the funeral sermon remains silent about the deceased or if ministers do not have a kind word to say when they describe the personal life of the deceased, which meant something in the world or in the church or for others. Jenssen regards remembering details from the life of the deceased *sub specie aeternitatis* as an expression of Christian love towards the deceased and bereaved. An absence

---

91. P. Sheppy, *Death Liturgy and Ritual*, vol. 1, 6: "What people ask for is to celebrate the individuality of the deceased." W. Carr, *Brief Encounters*, 30–31.

92. H. H. Jenssen, *Die kirchliche Handlungen*, 176: "The Christian testimony about God's *sklonenie* to each individual becomes untruthworthy, when the funeral preaching does not give enough space to the memory of the deceased. The sermon does not praise the deceased, but gives thanks to God for the life of the deceased."

of this expression, in his opinion calls into question the minister as a preacher of God's love. Jenssen goes as far as saying that excluding personal details for theological reasons may be theology, but certainly not Christian theology.[93] Jamnický also thinks that an absence of details about the deceased calls into question the approach and work of the minister,[94] and even that it causes the funeral sermon to lose its specific character because taking into consideration the deceased is what distinguishes it from church service sermons.[95]

Perry takes the opposite view when he claims that, if the deceased did not have an active faith life, then it is not necessary to mention that person in the sermon.[96] I regard this approach as unacceptable because the deceased is not mentioned in the funeral sermon merely as an illustration of the kerygmatic emphasis, or as reason for gratitude to God, but simply because the deceased was a person created in the image of God.

Responsibility of humans to God

In my opinion, an important argument for mentioning the deceased in the funeral sermon is the responsibility of humans to God. God gave humans the right to decide and responsibility for their decision. The death of a person is not the place to overlook the fact that God takes our responsibility seriously.

A formulation of the responsibility of humans before God is made more complicated as ministers cannot evaluate the fate of the deceased "from God's perspective." Especially in cases of people who did not live in a Christian way, ministers find themselves between two serious requirements: the need to express clearly that the responsibility of humans before God applies to the deceased and all others in attendance, and respect for the fact that God has the final word about humans. Naturally, if ministers are unable to express statements about the fate of the deceased from God's perspective, then fulfilling this task in connection to the deceased is not possible.

93. Ibid., 183.

94. J. Jamnický, *Evanjelické pohrebné kázne*, 79: "An example of such a mistake would be a funeral sermon on God's Word that could be used wherever and whenever, no matter whether it was for a devout Christian or an unbeliever. A mere objective message from the Word of God could be regarded in certain cases as showing a lack of love and compassion and in others, explained as neglect, a lack of investigation and an insult to the truth."

95. Ibid., 53.

96. L. M. Perry, *Manual for Biblical Preaching*, 189: "If the deceased man was unsaved, there is no need of reference to him. Give the declaration of one way of salvation through Christ and let the audience apply it to themselves."

However, ministers can fulfil this task in relation to those attending the funeral. When somebody is at the graveside of a loved one or acquaintance, the mortality of man is not perceived as a philosophical opinion but as a reality that touches everyone. Sooner or later we will answer to God for our attitude to him and for our way of life.

Reasons against Using Details about the Deceased

Arguments against mentioning the deceased in the funeral sermon stem from negative experiences when ministers did not do their job well and the sermon was either damaging because of an inadequate handling of thoughts about the deceased, or it was no longer preaching the Word of God. Stebler reflects on this: "It seems that an honest handling of the biography of a person is a sensitive and difficult subject. In everyday language, it is said: 'Funeral addresses are a pack of lies.'"[97]

As reasons against mentioning the deceased in the funeral sermon, the following three risks are mentioned: anthropocentrism, and a decline into praising the person; a lack of appropriate inspiration from the life of the deceased; and losing trustworthiness due to a false image of the deceased.

Anthropocentrism instead of proclaiming the Word

According to Jenssen, a fear of decline into praising the deceased sometimes leads to the recommendation to ignore the life of the deceased, or leave it to the biography that the bereaved will be responsible for and will read.[98] This objection, which points out the risk of anthropocentrism in the funeral sermon (meaning that God will not be preached but the focus will be on humanity),[99] must be respected and taken extremely seriously. Based on my observations, this risk is increased by a number of factors.

a.   The cultural tendency "to speak well of the dead," the tendency to evaluate the completed life of the person and express thanks for

---

97. Ch. Stebler, *Die drei Dimensionen*, 34.

98. H. H. Jenssen, *Die kirchliche Handlungen*, 182.

99. P. O. Axman and P. Aleš state: It is often said that funeral addresses should be mainly focused on a eulogy of the deceased; his deeds and good character traits should be emphasized as much as possible and given as an example for the people. This kind of understanding of the passing of a person, focused on his virtues and moral life, means giving him precedence over God himself. Out of people living on the earth, only the God-man Jesus Christ was without sin, and therefore he is the only example for all. The one starting point and centre point of every funeral address must be the Word of God and Christ's resurrection. *Homiletika*, 83.

what was good. As the funeral is not seen as being the place for an objective evaluation of the deceased, the speaker is likely to overlook any bad or weak points of the deceased and concentrate only on what was good. In a certain sense, there is a Christian attitude in this tendency because it attempts to look at the life of the deceased with love and forgiveness. Therefore, attention is deliberately not paid to the negatives – their judgement belongs to God – and the positives are noted, as gratitude will be expressed. The problem of this approach comes to the fore if it loses its Christian foundation in God – on true forgiveness and not a superficial social attitude – and a focus on God himself. Then all that remains is an attempt to say something nice about the deceased, without any relationship to the truth.

b. Theologically badly handled gratitude. After the death of someone who lived a good Christian life, Christians realize that the source of the good they received through the deceased was God. Therefore, they desire to give thanks to God for that good. If ministers do not stick to this line of thinking, their sermon can descend into praising the person, and paradoxically the loss of a place for God.

c. The loss of the biblical message. Where ministers lose faith in the significance of God's Word for the situation of loss, they will search for other tools to comfort the grieving, for example praising the values of the deceased. This can then lead to talking about the deceased and not fulfilling the task of bringing the healing words of God to the lives of the funeral congregation.

A lack of appropriate inspiration from the life of the deceased

Ministers of large churches often bury deceased people whom they did not know at all. The requirement of a personalized approach either exposes these ministers to excessive stress[100] or exposes them to the risk of making comments based on general assumptions that sound like personal notes. In the first case, it would increase the workload and difficulty of preparing for the ceremony, and in the second case, it puts the trustworthiness of the minister at risk. Therefore,

---

100. H. H. Jenssen states that because of fear that ministers will have a small quantity or low quality information about the life of the deceased, he recommends that occasionally they ignore the life of the deceased. But, according to Jenssen, there are some very serious objections to this approach. *Die Kirchliche Handlungen*, 182.

it is possible to understand an attempt to exclude personal comments from the sermon as an attempt to protect the minister.

A loss of trustworthiness due to a false image of the deceased

A lack of information about the deceased is clearly not related to the funeral sermon becoming too like a eulogy described by T. G. Long,[101] because in the example he gives, it is clear that the minister twisted the facts. My observations show that a lack of information about the deceased means ministers are unable to filter the testimonies they hear. A minister with whom I spoke after a funeral about his good homiletical use of details about the deceased told me: "When I was younger, I got into full flow in a sermon and said more about the deceased than was really truthful. Afterwards I was heavily criticized for it." Several years ago, I came across an exceptional case in southern Slovakia of the funeral sermon being damaged by becoming too like a eulogy due to a lack of information about the deceased. The bereaved informed the minister that their grandmother had died. He accepted the death certificate and prepared the funeral. He buried her as if she had been a model Christian. Only after the funeral did he find out that he had been thinking about the grandmother from the other side of the family who was also close to death, but he had just buried a woman who was not a Christian and had a lot of unmistakable deficiencies. If he had more information, he would not have forced those in attendance to ask whether he had any idea what he was talking about.

My Position

On the basis of these points, I will attempt to express my position. The Roman Catholic recommendation that a funeral homily should not be a eulogy[102]

---

101. T. G. Long refers to the problem of the serious damage done to the funeral sermon through the addition of features of a eulogy, which is convincingly and clearly portrayed by studying the funeral sermon of Jacques Bénigne Bossuet (1627–1704) for the funeral of Anne Gonzaga, "a social schemer, whose behind the scenes tactics, hateful personality, and public offences where a hot topic of conversation in Paris." According to Long, in this funeral sermon Bossuet "transformed the princess from a sinner into a saint," which may seem to be interesting to those present as well as loving to the deceased person. But in this way the minister ruins his work as a minister. Long evaluates it with the words: "According to all reports, Bossuet's listeners at the funeral were moved by his oration but doubted his facts." T. G. Long, "O Sing to Me of Heaven: Preaching at Funerals," *Journal for Preachers* 29, no. 3 (Easter 2006): 20.

102. "Congregation for Divine Worship and the Discipline of the Sacraments," *Homiletic Directory*, 74, 155. The Order of Christian Funerals articulates concisely the purpose and the meaning of the homily at a funeral. In the light of the Word of God, while keeping in mind the fact that the homily must avoid the form and style of a eulogy (cf. 141), "priests are to keep in

seems to be designed to maintain a biblical emphasis and to prevent mistakes which occur when praising the person replaces preaching the Word. A Protestant theologian can completely agree with this approach and endorse it as a foundational principle for ministers of reformed churches. The arguments against including details about the deceased contain warnings about serious risks. But the exclusion of these details also presents risks. Rudolf Bohren highlights them with his declaration: "There are ministers who attempt to avoid trivializing their funeral addresses by preaching 'pure gospel' and are not influenced by the case in any way. If some ministers are sinning by not honouring God, then here they are sinning by not honouring their neighbour, and they must ask the question whether the 'pure' gospel, which is seemingly correctly exegeted, speaks to every situation."[103] With this Bohren demonstrates that the risk does not arise from the existence of details about the deceased person but from the absence of a responsible approach to the funeral sermon. Therefore, I hold the opinion that, based on what the funeral sermon is in essence, there does not arise any necessity to exclude the deceased from the sermon.[104]

A Christian funeral address should be a sermon which should place the deceased, those grieving, and the whole funeral congregation before God and bring his Word into the setting of saying farewell. If this task is abandoned, it would result in a loss in a number of areas. Assuming a theocentric approach to the funeral sermon does not lead to the requirement that the deceased is not mentioned at all. If ministers preach Christ and bring a message about him to the situation of loss and searching for a new orientation, they have a safe theological-anthropological framework for making appropriate use of details about the deceased, which reduces the risk of any kind of misuse.[105]

---

mind with delicate sensitivity not only the identity of the deceased and the circumstances of the death, but also the grief of the bereaved and their needs for a Christian life" ("Introduction of the Order of Christian Funerals 18 [Latin edition]"), *Homiletic Directory*, Vatican City, 2014.

103. R. Bohren, *Unsere Kasualpraxis – eine missionarische Gelegenheit?* (Munich: Kaiser, 1968), 20, in Ch. Stebler, *Die drei Dimensionen*, 39.

104. Both the side arguing for the use of details about the deceased and the opposite side use arguments based on the influence on the trustworthiness of the message. This seems to relativize the meaning of the parameter. In reality both sides are right – avoiding the deceased calls the biblical message into question, and bad use of the details of the deceased calls ministers into question, and indirectly their message.

105. P. Sheppy states, "When we speak of the dead at the funeral, we speak by reference to Christ the firstborn from the dead (Col 1:17). The funeral rite which fails to make this connection is, in my judgement, inadequately Christian." *Death Liturgy and Ritual*, vol. 1, 65.

Therefore, I am able to recommend making appropriate homiletical use of details about the deceased.

Requirements for References to the Deceased

In connection with the function of the funeral sermon, it was said that the personality of the deceased should be reflected in the funeral, at least in some basic features. This does not mean that this requirement can be met by combining any sermon that touches on the topic of the meaning of life, mortality, etc., with a series of thoughts about the deceased. What should be attempted is an appropriate linkage of the topic to the details of the specific case and its appropriate pastoral application, if it is possible, in the sermon.[106]

Truth

The minister must pay attention to truthfulness both from the human perspective, meaning verifiable information, and from God's perspective, not predict God's verdict about the deceased. Therefore all statements must be given as expressions of human evaluation and not God's.

1. Truthfulness from a human perspective, verifiable information and the credibility of the minister. Without wishing to doubt the spiritual and human quality of the deceased, I recommend only using facts that have been verified a number of times.[107] This is because the details the minister gives about the deceased are the easiest thing for those in attendance to check and function as a measure of how credible the minister is.

    If the listeners hear ten statements about the deceased, and if in their opinion eight of them are false, then they conclude that they can only trust the minister 20 percent of the time. This has very serious consequences for the proclamation of the gospel, because this measure is transferred from the verifiable field of the evaluation of the deceased to the unverifiable field (for the listeners) of the

---

106. ČCE (Evangelical Church of Czech Brethren) in their agenda (*Agenda ČCE*, 195) express the following: "It is best before the sermon (which is its usual place or added to other addresses) or spoken by the funeral director or a presbyter. From the point of view of where to place these references, it is possible to make use of various parts of the ceremony: (1) the sermon; (2) in the Lutheran tradition during the committal – as concise overview of the life of the deceased; or (3) as a part of a block of speeches."

107. B. Chapell, *Christ-Centered Preaching*, 345: "Avoid exaggeration of anyone's good life." Similarly, *Agenda ČCE*, 195: references to the deceased "should be truthful."

testimony about God. The level of truthfulness about the deceased becomes the final measure of the truthfulness of ministers in their kerygmatic testimony, and in this way ministers can seriously damage their position as preachers. The listeners who hear the gospel are led to think that it is not necessary to think about his words, because the minister cannot be believed. Therefore, this kind of approach is extremely risky, and no other benefit that it may bring can balance it up.

2.   Truthfulness from God's perspective, not predicting God's verdict. On the basis of Krusche's fourth proposition,[108] I agree that ministers cannot judge that the deceased went to heaven or hell.[109] Only God knows the life of the humans, the opportunities they had, and how they responded to the chances God gave them. Therefore, every funeral sermon must proclaim that human lives are judged by God. But this cannot remove our confidence to say farewell to a deceased Christian in the hope of the resurrection. I also agree with the opinion of Bryan Chapell that ministers should not give false hope when they know that the deceased was not a Christian.[110] They should speak about the blessings of the gospel, which are shared by those who profess faith in Jesus Christ, without saying that it applies to the deceased.

3.   Truthful statements, an expression of human rather than God's evaluation. Jenssen points out that when ministers choose events

---

108. W. Krusche, "Unsere Predigt am Sarg," in *Schritte und Markierungen* (Berlin: Evangelische Verlagsanstalt, 1972), 84–108 quoted in J. Smolík, *Radost ze slova,* 151: "4/ God gifted the deceased a certain length of time to live; in it he should have in faithful obedience embraced salvation through baptism. To what extent the deceased understood this salvation, the minister is in principle unable to assess. The specific facts of the completed life should be considered from the perspective of being called to faith, obedience and gratitude."

109. H. W. Robinson, J. E. Means, and P. D. Borden state, "It is completely inappropriate to suggest that the deceased has gone to a place of eternal damnation. This might be a true statement, but the preacher is not God and cannot know the heart of the person. Much better is the approach that all of us are mortal and need to deal with the questions of eternity." "Guidelines for Difficult Funerals," in *A Contemporary Handbook for Weddings and Funerals and Other Occasions,* 212.

110. Chapell, *Christ-Centered Preaching,* 344. This theme is also reflected on by Jamnický, *Evanjelické pohrebné kázne,* 89: (About those in bondage to sin) "It requires great pastoral wisdom and tact on the part of the minister to not ignore or deny the truth, to not offend the grieving relatives who are at this moment very sensitive and can easily become embittered, and to not provide *Ohrenschmaus* (ear candy) for the indifferent, insensitive onlookers, who often appear on mass at funerals."

from the life of the deceased, they are evaluating the deceased's life.[111] Therefore, it is essential that ministers are aware that when assessing the value of events, human achievements, and ways of behaving, it is possible to be in error and that their evaluation is not identical to God's.[112] This is why Jenssen contends that ministers should continually repeat phrases like "to the extent we can correctly see . . ." or "based on a human assessment, it is possible to say . . ." He recommends this approach because he expects that human opinions often need to be revised *sub specie aeternitatis*, and this stimulates the funeral congregation to fruitful thinking about the life of the deceased and the meaning of human life.[113]

Love

Ministers should demonstrate love to their neighbours in the funeral sermon. The teaching that if "I have not love" (1 Cor 13:1b, 2b, 3b), "I am nothing" (v. 2b) should be applied here. If ministers want to think deeply about how they should express love in their testimony about the deceased, a helpful structure to use is 1 Corinthians 13:4–7. Love does not mean turning a blind eye to failings, but even the average attendee at the funeral is able to judge whether ministers speak about the deceased with respect and Christian love or whether what they say is religiously pretentious and condemned the possible failings of the deceased.

In positive testimonies, love is expressed through respect to the deceased and as thankfulness for the deceased's contributions. In connection with negative expressions, it can be stated that love will never defame the deceased. Funeral sermons are not the place to express moralizing opinions about the deceased, not even in cases where the deceased lived a disorderly life or was regarded by the community and closest associates as downright evil.[114] Jamincký correctly summarizes that, "It is not allowed to defame at the graveside, because

---

111. H. H. Jenssen, *Die kirchliche Handlungen,* in *Handbuch der Praktischen Theologie* vol 2, 184.

112. Also, according to Ch. Stebler, it must be clear when evaluating the deceased that it is not God's evaluation but only human and provisional. *Die drei Dimensionen,* 44.

113. H. H. Jenssen, *Die kirchliche Handlungen,* in *Handbuch der Praktischen Theologie, vol. 2,* 184–185.

114. In the opposite case of extremely good relationships, ministers should proceed in such a way that their statements about the deceased and bereaved do not create feelings of rejection in those who were unable to gain the bereaved's favour.

that offends and does not solve anything."[115] Using a reference to Nierbergall, Jamincký criticizes the idea of revenge in the form of insinuations about the deceased, which a socially healthy and normal Christian cannot even imagine and would regard as completely unacceptable.[116]

The christological context of the testimony about the deceased
Mentions of the deceased in a Christian funeral sermon must have a christological context, meaning they must express the fact that everyone has sinned against God and needs his forgiveness.[117] This applies to people who were unable to live exemplary lives, but it is especially important at the funerals of excellent Christians. Ministers cannot express even the most striking examples from the life of the deceased in such a way that they entitle the deceased to eternal life, because that is God's gift by grace.[118] Otherwise the subject of the message becomes the deceased and not God's actions in Christ. This type of testimony calls into question the theological testimony about redemption in Christ.[119] On the other hand, with cases of strong Christians, ministers are able to point to God's work in the life of the deceased as a source of the good which benefited the deceased's social circle.

Axman and Aleš point to another dimension of the christological context when they speak about the defeat of death by Christ through his resurrection, which they see as the starting point for funeral sermons. Only after that is

---

115. J. Jamnický, *Evanjelické pohrebné kázne*, 91.

116. Ibid., 83, quoting F. Niebergall, *Die Kasualrede* (Göttingen: Vandenhoeck & Ruprecht, 1905), 168, in J. Jamnický, *Evanjelické pohrebné kázne*. "Not anywhere near reaching the depths of priestly shame and disgrace, that those ministers bring on the priesthood, if through easily observable insinuations they take revenge at the graveside for various personal offences, inconveniences, etc. which the deceased or his relatives caused him."

117. *Agenda ČCE*, 195: Remembrance of the deceased "should . . . remember that everyone has transgressed before God, and is reliant on his forgiveness."

118. Similarly Perry states, "Avoid exaggeration of the good life lived by a deceased Christian." *Manual for Biblical Preaching*, 190.

119. Eberhard Winkler states: "In the history of occasional preaching, talking about the deceased has always been viewed as the most difficult problem. Teaching about justification, by which the Lutheran self-understanding as a church stands and falls, is refuted when the impression is made that people could be accepted by God due to their good lives. Mr X. never went to a church service, never indicated that faith meant something to him, but he was a hardworking man who lived for his family; he was friendly and considerate to his neighbours and colleagues. And apart from that, since his baptism he never left the church. It seems that this is sufficient for him to be allocated a place in heaven." *Tore zum Leben: Taufe – Konfirmation – Trauung – Bestattung* (Neukirchen: Vluyn, 1995), 185n, in Ch. Stebler, *Die drei Dimensionen*, 35.

J. Jamnický states something similar, that ministers evaluate the life of the deceased using civil criteria, thereby losing a spiritual perspective "and then follows the unfortunate conclusion, that God will definitely be gracious to them." *Evanjelické pohrebné kázne*, 87.

it possible to "evaluate" the personal merit of the deceased and praise good Christian traits.[120]

When to not use details of the deceased

If ministers do not know the deceased and they cannot obtain trustworthy information, it is better if they do not attempt a personal approach and do not expose themselves to the risk of non-objective or even false testimony. Similar advice can also be found for the case of funerals where people during their lifetime did not manifest as Christians. Chapell states, "Preachers in older times said that when preaching a funeral for one who was not known as a believer they would 'Read the man's facts, then preach the Lord's gospel'; i.e., let people know whose funeral it is by some personal reference, but then move on to preach the gospel without judging whether the one applied to the other. This is still good advice."[121] If they include an embellishment of the deceased, the listeners might not regard it as bad, but it would damage their credibility and consequently the biblical message.[122] Therefore, ministers need to set criteria for the use of details about the deceased which will not be risky but support the fulfilment of the task of the funeral sermon.

---

120. P. O. Axman and P. Aleš, *Homiletika*, 82.

121. B. Chapell, *Christ-Centered Preaching*, 344.

122. The opposite was experienced by a civil funeral celebrant who told me that at one funeral, he gave a number of positive testimonies about the deceased which he had not verified, and someone in attendance reacted out loud saying: "That isn't true!"

Conclusion

Proclaiming God's Word in a funeral sermon is not just subjectively a stressful part of the work of ministers, but objectively it represents a very demanding part of their ministry. Most of the congregation find it difficult to listen due to being burdened by their loss, and others represent a challenge because of their attitude to God and the church. Funeral congregations are very diverse, and ministers should set different aims for each group. All of this is to be done in the relatively short range of six hundred to nine hundred words. Therefore, it is necessary to use this limited space for communication very economically, and both what ministers say and do not say must lead to fulfilment of the homiletical purposes.

The difficult surroundings, as they have been described in this publication, require that ministers take a professional approach. The content must be grounded in the biblical disciplines, and answers to the questions that define the context of the listeners must be found on the basis of interdisciplinary discussion with non-theological experts. Among these it is mainly psychologists who help to understand the situation of the listeners. Therefore, it is necessary to develop a critical approach to current practice and with gratitude note all positive inspirations and make use of them for building on the best results of current practice. Ministers must also have the courage to classify all phenomena which could complicate the effective communication of the gospel in the already complicated context of a funeral.

This publication attempts to resolve questions about funeral sermons in an ecumenical context, which at the same time causes problems. This is manifested not only in terminology (Protestants: funeral sermon – Roman Catholics: funeral homily), but also in statements that are based on soteriological beliefs. In resolving questions about formalities, I could have been too influenced by my previous work with Lutheran approaches. Despite this, I believe it is worth joining forces ecumenically in the search for effective approaches to the question of proclaiming the gospel at funerals and to serve each other in ecumenical discussion through asking questions which exist already.

The division of this work into chapters reflects the way I ask questions. First it deals with the question of funeral sermons in general (ch. 1). This section searches for ways to define funeral sermons from different starting points and demonstrates where a funeral sermon has standard homiletical characteristics and which characteristics are conditioned by its specific context. Next, detailed attention is paid to the homiletical situation of the funeral (ch. 2), because I hold the view that the significance of current funeral preaching is or can be in danger from an insufficient consideration of the listeners' situation. In specific situations, this can be an obstacle to secular people engaging with the biblical message that they hear.

Arising from the significance of the homiletical situation for the funeral sermon, I observe that it is necessary to increase the effectiveness of the funeral sermon by strengthening the pastoral contact of ministers with the bereaved. This remains as an observation, and, for a number of reasons, suggestions that could be realized are not given.

Also, it is necessary to define the purpose of a funeral sermon (ch. 3) from a number of perspectives to avoid it being one-sided. It is guaranteed that the church service purposes – glorifying God and bowing before him – will be discussed, but also pastoral and evangelistic purposes which must be developed with sensitivity for the ecumenical context of the proceedings.

The homiletical process of the funeral sermon (ch. 4) is in essence identical to the homiletical process of preparing a standard church service sermon. In practice, there are differences whose existence are difficult to justify theologically. Therefore, it is necessary to search for ways that would, at least from time to time, enable ministers to receive qualified feedback on their ministry and encouragement about what they are doing well. Where there is need for improvement, it is necessary to search for what it is possible to do about reconciling homiletical requirements and the constraints in practice. Time-consuming tasks including exegesis of the text and thinking about its application to the situation of today could be supported by homiletical-exegetical aids, analysis of the quality of funeral preaching from individual church traditions, and activities as a part of a minister's lifelong learning. Otherwise there is the risk that ministers who conduct a large number of funerals will fall into a routine approach and take material from collections of funeral sermons in an uncreative way, which stunts their professional growth.

A problem of funeral preaching that I observed is that its current state is socially acceptable, and I repeatedly noticed that ministers do not feel the need to pay significant attention to this area. If the potential of this ministry is to be fully realized, it requires a relatively large amount of personal and time commitment by ministers who often already feel overwhelmed by their workload. But by pursuing this route, it is possible to gain something of significant value. The bereaved can experience real help from the church and not only better process their loss, but also in a key moment of life deepen their relationship with God and the church. The church can through this ministry gain respect from non-Christians when in the words of Jesus it is willing to go the extra mile with someone.

Bibliography

Agenda českobratrské církve evangelické. Praha: Synodní rada ČCE, 1983.

Agenda Církve československé husitské. Praha: Blahoslav, 1997.

Atkinson, David, J. et al. *New Dictionary of Christian Ethics and Pastoral Theology.* Downers Grove, IL; Leicester, UK: InterVarsity Press, 1995.

Axman, P. O., and Aleš, P. *Homiletika.* Olomouc: Pravoslavná Bohoslovecká Fakulta Prešovské Univerzity v Prešově, Detašované pracoviště v Olomouci, 2003.

Blackwood, A. W. *The Funeral.* Grand Rapids: Baker Books, 1972.

Blumenthal-Barby, Kay a kol. *Opatrovanie ťažko chorých a umierajúcich.* Martin: Vydavateľstvo Osveta, n.p.: 1988.

Bohren, R. *Predigtlehre.* München: Kaiser, 1980.

———. *Unsere Kasualpraxis – eine missionarische Gelegenheit?* Munich: Kaiser, 1968.

Brádňanská, N. *Pastorálny postoj k smrti človeka so zameraním na zomieranie detí a dospievajúcich.* Bratislava: Inštitút vzdelávania Evanjelickej cirkví metodistickej vo Vydavateľstve ECM spol. s.r.o., 1999.

Breit, H., and M. Seitz. *Beerdigung. Calwer Predigthilfen.* Stuttgart: Calwer, 1974.

Bukovský, M. *Kritická analýza úloh pohrebnej kázne. Diplomová práca.* Banská Bystrica: KETM PF UMB, 2006.

Carr, W. *Brief Encounters: Pastoral Ministry through Baptism, Weddings and Funerals.* Revised edition. London: SPCK, 1994.

———. *Handbook of Pastoral Studies: Learning and Practising Christian Ministry.* London: SPCK, 1997.

Chapell, B. *Christ-Centered Preaching: Redeeming the Expository Sermon.* Grand Rapids: Baker, 2000.

Chapman, M. E. "The Authentic Word in the Face of Death: Reflections on Preaching at Funerals." *Currents in Theology and Mission* 22, no. 1 (Fall 1995): 38–42.

"Congregation for Divine Worship and the Discipline of the Sacraments." *Homiletic Directory.* Vatican City, 2014.

Crabb, Larry. *Effective Biblical Counseling: A Model for Helping Caring Christians Become Capable Counselors.* Grand Rapids, MI: Zondervan, 1977.

Cruse Bereavement Care. *Bereavement Care in Practice: The Cruse Approach to Working with Bereaved People.* Richmond, UK: Cruse Bereavement Care, 2004.

———. *Bereavement: Support When You Need It Most.* Thematic sheet, Death by Suicide. Richmond: Cruse Bereavement Care, 2013.

Cullman, O. *Christologie Nového Zákona.* Praha: Kalich, 1976.

Dillon, R. J. "The Unavoidable Discomforts of Preaching about Death." *Worship* 57, no 6 (November 1983): 486–496.

Donnelly, P., and G. Connon. *Guidelines for the Immediate Response to Children and Families in Traumatic Death Situations. Professionals Guide.* Belfast: The Royal Hospitals, 2003.

Duthie, C., ed. *Resurrection and Immortality: A Selection from the Drew Lectures on Immortality.* London: Samuel Bagster & Sons, 1979.

Estep, W. R. *Příběh křtěnců. Radikálové Evropské reformace.* Praha: Bratrská jednota baptistů, 1991.

Fabián, A. *Utrpenie má aj iný rozmer.* Prešov: Vydavateľstvo Michala Vaška, 1999.

Fee, G. D. *New Testament Exegesis: A Handbook for Students and Pastors.* Louisville: Westminster John Knox, 2002.

Filkins, K. *Comfort Those Who Mourn: How to Preach Personalized Funeral Messages.* Joplin, MO: College Press Publishing, 1992.

Filo, J. *Pohľady do neba. Kázne, príhovory a rozlúčky pri pohreboch a pietnych príležitostiach.* Vydavateľstvo Michala Vaška, Prešov, 2004.

Foltynovský, J. *Duchovní řečnictví.* Nákladem vlastním, 1927.

Gelineau, J. "L´homélie, forme pléniere de la predication." In *Maison Dieu.* Paris: Les editions du Cerf, 1965.

Hanes, P. *Interaktívny úvod do filozofie pre teológov.* Banská Bystrica: PF UMB, 2003.

Havránek, A. *Úvahy o pastýřské péči.* Praha: Rada Církve bratrské, 1986.

Horský, R., and M. Durchánek. *O svátostech a o křesťanském pohřbu.* Praha: Blahoslav, 1976.

Horton, P. M. a kol. *Systematická teológie.* Albrechtice: Křesťanský život, 2001.

Hošek, P. *Na cestě dialogu. Křesťanská víra v pluralitě náboženství.* Praha: Návrat domů, 2005.

Hughes, R. *A Trumpet in Darkness: Preaching to Mourners.* Philadelphia: Fortress Press, 1985.

Hürlimann, C. *Ich will mit dir gehen. Vom Umgang mit Trauernden.* Zürich: Theologischer Verlag, 1981.

———. *Sterben – auch mein Weg.* Zürich: Theologischer Verlag, 1981.

———. *Von Meiner Seite gerissen.* Zürich: Theologischer Verlag, 1981.

Hybels, B., H. Robinson, and S. Briscoe. *Mastering Contemporary Preaching.* Portland, OR: Multnomah, 1989.

Jacoš, J. Prot. *Homiletika.* Prešov: PBF PU, 2003.

Jamnický, J. *Evanjelické pohrebné kázne. Homiletická úvaha.* Liptovský sv. Mikuláš: Tranoscius, 1927.

Jenssen, H. H. "Die Kirchlichen Handlungen." In *Handbuch der Praktischen Theologie,* volume 2. Berlin: Evangelische Verlagsanstalt, 1979.

Jeschke, B. J. *Nauka o kázání, Homiletika.* Praha: KEBF edice Kalich, 1971.

Jurko, J. *Verím, že môj Vykupiteľ žije. Pomôcka k pohrebným príhovorom.* Kapušany: Ing. Štefánia Beňová - Bens, 2000.

Kacianová, N. *Problematika žiaľu pozostalého človeka. Pastorálne výzvy a teologické riešenia. [Dizertačná práca].* Bratislava: EBF UK, 2008.

Kavanagh, Aidan. *Made Not Born: New Perspectives on Christian Initiation.* Notre Dame: University of Notre Dame Press, 1976.

Kišš, I. *Nádej nad hrobom, 1–4. časť.* Pohrebné kázne, Bratislava, 1995–96, vlastný náklad.

Kolle, E. *Grabreden. Für die Geistliche Rede.* Gütersloh: C. Bertelsmann Verlag, 1938.

Koštiaľ, R., and J. Michalko. *Malá dogmatika.* Liptovský Mikuláš: Tranoscius v Cirkevnom vydavateľstve, Bratislava, 1986.

Křivohlavý, J. *Pastorální péče.* Praha: ETS, 2000.

Kubíková, J. *Kažte evangelium: metodická pomůcka pro kazatele.* Praha: Blahoslav, 1992.

Kübler-Ross, E. *On Death and Dying: What the Dying Have to Teach Doctors, Nurses, Clergy and Their Own Families.* London and New York: Routledge, 2009.

Ladd, G. E. *Teológie Nového Zákona. Podle G. L. Ladda zpracoval Karel Taschner.* Praha: ETS, 2003.

Liguš, Ján. *Dogmaticum* – preprint, KETM. Banská Bystrica: KETM PF UMB, 2003.

Lindemann, E. "Symptomatology and Management of Acute Grief." In *American Journal of Psychiatry* 101: 141–148.

Long, T. G. "O Sing to Me of Heaven: Preaching at Funerals." In *Journal for Preachers* 29, no. 3 (Easter 2006): 21–26.

———. "The Funeral: Changing Patterns and Teachable Moments." *Journal for Preachers* (Easter 1996): 3–8.

Louw, J. P., and Eugene Albert Nida, eds. *Greek-English Lexicon of the New Testament: Based on Semantic Domain*, volume 1. New York: United Bible Societies, 1989.

Luebering, C. *Helping a Child Grieve and Grow.* St. Meinrad, IN: Abbey Press, 1990.

Malphurs, A., and K. Willhite, eds. *A Contemporary Handbook for Weddings and Funerals and Other Occasions.* Grand Rapids: Kregel, 2003.

Masarik, A. *Analýza nekérygmatických komponentov pohrebných kázní prof. Igora Kišša.* Banská Bystrica: PF UMB, 2008.

Melloh, J. A. "Homily or Eulogy? The Dilemma of Funeral Preaching." *Worship* 67, no. 6 (1993): 502–518.

Michalko, J. *Kázňové smery.* Liptovský Mikuláš: Tranoscius v Cirkevnom nakladateľstve Bratislava, 1955.

———. *Praktická exegéza.* Liptovský Mikuláš: Tranoscius v Cirkevnom nakladateľstve Bratislava, 1977.

Moltmann, J. *In the End – the Beginning.* London: SMC, 2004.

Niebauer, J. *Liturgie.* Praha: Úzká rada Jednoty bratrské, 1959.

Packer, J. I. *Evangelizace a Boží svrchovanost.* Praha: Návrat domů, 2000.

Parkes, C. M. *Bereavement: Studies of Grief in Adult Life.* 3rd edition. Philadelphia: Taylor & Francis, 2001, (First edition 1972).

Perry, L. M. *A Manual for Biblical Preaching.* Grand Rapids: Baker, 1992.

Petrík, J. M. *Pohrebná agenda*. Liptovský Mikuláš: Tranoscius, v Cirkevnom nakladateľstve Bratislava 1983.

Piesne nádeje. Bratislava: Ústredná rada starších Apoštolskej cirkví na Slovensku v Cirkevnom nakladateľstve Bratislava, 1987. (A book of funeral songs in the Slovak Republic, published by a local church.)

Piper, J. *Božia zvrchovanosť v kázaní*. Bratislava: Návrat Domov, 2000.

Pohl, A. *Anleitung zum Predigen: ein Arbeitsheft für Predigthelfer*. Wuppertal und Kasel: Oncken Verlag, 1979.

Pohřební obřady. Kostelní Vydří: Karmelitánské nakladatelství. Praha: Liturgický inštitút, 1999.

Pokorný, P. *Úvod do exegeze*. Praha: Kalich, 1979.

Robinson, H. W. *Biblical Preaching*. Grand Rapids: Baker, 1980.

Robinson, H. W., and C. B. Larson, eds. *The Art and Craft of Biblical Preaching: A Comprehensive Resource for Today's Communicators*. Grand Rapids: Zondervan, 2005.

Rummage, S. N. "Redemptive Sermons for Weddings and Funerals: When the Sermon Is the Last Thing on Your Hearers' Minds." In *The Art and Craft of Biblical Preaching: A Comprehensive Resource for Today's Communicators*, edited by H. Robinson and C. B. Larson. Grand Rapids: Zondervan, 2005.

Rutrle, O. *Křesťanská služba slovem*. Praha: Blahoslav, 1952.

Ryrie, C. C. *Základy teológie*. Třinec: Biblos, 1994.

Šefranko, M., and R. Cingeľ. *Potešujte sa vospolok týmito slovami. Zbierka pohrebných príhovorov evanjelických a.v.duchovných*. Bratislava/Prešov: ZED, 2009.

———. *Príručka pre zborové služby*. [p.l.]: Vydané pre vnútornú potrebu Bratskej jednoty baptistov v ČSFR, [p.a.].

Senior, D., and C. Stuhlmueller. *Biblické základy misie*. Levice: JPK, 2002.

Sheppy, P. *Death Liturgy and Ritual. Volume 1, A Pastoral and Liturgical Theology*. Aldershot, UK: Ashgate, 2003.

———. *Death Liturgy and Ritual. Volume 2, A Commentary on Liturgical Texts*. Aldershot, UK: Ashgate, 2004.

———. *In Sure and Certain Hope: Liturgies, Prayers and Readings for Funerals and Memorials*. Norwich, UK: Canterbury Press, 2003.

Šimkovic, J. *Věřím tela z mrtvých vzkříšení! Výber pohrebných rečí, ktoré pri rozličných príležitostiach povedal Ján Šimkovic*. Ružomberok: Tranoscius, 1921.

Smolík, Josef. *Radost ze slova. Náčrt homiletiky*. Praha: Kalich, 1983.

Šoltésová, V. "Determinanty rozvoja religiozity Rómov na Slovensku." In Zborník zmedzinárodného ekumenického vedeckého sympózia "Človek v núdzi," which took place 2–3 May 2006 at the TF Katolícka univerzita in Košice. Košice: Ekumenické spoločenstvo cirkví na území mesta Košice, 2006.

———. "Využitie rómskeho prekladu Písma v homiletickej činnosti cirkví na východnom Slovensku." In *Homiletická činnosť cirkví a kvalita súčasného života*.

Zborník prednášok z vedeckej teologickej konferencie. Banská Bystrica: KETM PF UMB a ZEC vo vyd. Trian, p. r. o., 2009.

Souček, J. B. *Řecko-český slovník k Novému zákonu.* Praha: KEBF, 1973.

Spurgeon, C. H. *Lectures to My Students.* London: Passmore & Alabaster, Paternoster Buildings, 1877.

———. *Ratschläge für Prediger.* 21 Vorlesungen. Wuppertal und Kassel: Oncken Verlag, 1992.

Stanček, Ľ. *Pohrebné homílie.* Spišská Kapitula – Spišské Podhradie: Kňazský seminár biskupa Jána Vojtaššáka, 2003.

Stebler, C. *Die drei Dimensionen der Bestattungspredigt, Theologie, Biographie und Trauergemeinde.* Zürich: Theologisker Verlag, 2006.

Sugden, H. F. and W. W. Wiersbe. *Confident Pastoral Leadership: Practical Solutions to Perplexing Problems.* Chicago: Moody Press, 1973.

Šuráb, M. *Terapeutický rozmer homílie.* Bratislava: Vydavateľstvo spolku slovenských spisovateľov, spol. p.r.o. pre Rímskokatolícku cyrilometodskú bohosloveckú fakultu UK, 2008.

———. *Impulzy. Myšlienky k pohrebným homíliám.* Nitra: Kňazský seminár sv. Gorazda v Nitre, 1998.

Taročkova, T. *Životné straty a smútenie.* Bratislava: FF UK, 2005.

Theroux, P. *The Book of Eulogies: A Collection of Memorial Tributes, Poetry, Essays, and Letters of Condolence.* New York: Scribner, 1997.

Van Dam, W. C. *Mŕtvi nezomierajú.* Bratislava: ECM, 1994.

Van Gennep, A. *The Rites of Passage.* Reprint. London: Routledge, 2004.

Vrablec, J. *Homiletika.* Trnava: SSV, v Cirkevnom nakladateľstve. Bratislava, 1987.

Vrablec, J., and A. Fabián. *Homiletika I.–II. základná a materiálna.* Trnava: SSV, 2001.

Vyznání a řád Církve bratrské. (Church document from one of the free evangelical churches in the Czech Republic.) Praha: Rada Církve bratrské, 2005.

Wallis, C. L. *The Funeral Encyclopedia: A Source Book.* New York, Evanston, and London: Harper & Row, 1953.

Wantuła, A. *Zarys homiletyki ewangelickiej.* Warszawa: Vydawnictwo Zviastun, 1974.

Worden, J. W. *Grief Counseling and Grief Therapy: A Handbook for the Mental Health Practitioner.* New York: Springer, 2009.

Wray, Judith H. "Preaching Life in the Face of Death." *Living Pulpit* 4, no. 3 (Jl-S 1995): 40.

Zemko, P. *Homiletické směrnice. Z dějin homiletiky na Moravě, v Čechách a na Slovensku.* Trnava: Dobrá kniha, 2007.

Recommended Literature

Adámek, František. *Ve vzkříšení k životu věčnému. In: Český zápas.* Praha: Týdeník církve Československé, Jr. 52, Nr. 44, 30 Oct 1969.

Berger, H. *Die christliche Botschaftvon Tod und Auferstehung und ihre Verkündigung am Grabe, Habilitation work*. Berlin, 10 Jun 1963.

Bošmanský, K. *Človek vo svetle pastorálnej medicíny a medicínskej etiky*. Spišské Podhradie: Kňazský seminár biskupa Jána Vojtaššáka, 1996.

Brabec, Ladislav. *Křesťanská thanatologie*. Praha: GEMMA89, 1991.

Foltynovský, J. *Liturgika*. Olomouc: Matice cyrilometodějská, 1936.

Frankl, V. E. *Man's Search for Meaning*. Boston: Beacon Press, 2006.

Hanes, P. *Teológia katastrofy podľa Knihy Jóbovej*. Banská Bystrica: PF UMB, 2008.

———. "Teodicea a Jóbova katastrofa." In *Evanjelikálny teoogický* časopip, 34–40. Banská Bystrica: PF UMB 2005/1.

Kašparů J. M. *Homiletické trivium*. Olomouc: Matice cyrilometodějská, 2001.

Kierdorf, W. *Laudatio funebris: Interpretationen und Untersuchungen zur Entwicklung der römischen Leichenrede. Beiträge zur Klassischen Philologie 106*. Meisenheim a. Glan: Hain, 1980.

Křivohlavý, J. *Sdílení naděje*. Praha: Návrat domů, 1997.

———. *Mít pro co žít*. Praha: Návrat domů, 1994.

Nemčeková, M., K. Žiaková, and M.Palenčár. *Človek medzi životom a smrťou*. Martin: JLF UK, 1996.

Pribula, M., and G. Paľa. *Stručne o komunikácii nielen pre teológov*. Prešov: Pro communio, o.z., 2006.

Ratzinger, J. *Eschatology: Death and eternal Life*. Washington, DC: The Catholic University of America Press, 1988.

Roth, U. *Die Beerdigungsansprache*. Gütersloh: Kaiser, 2002.

Schiller, K. E. *Sterben – und was dann?* Wien-Linz-Passau: Veritas-Verlag, 1979.

Simajchl, L., J. Daněk, and M. Klisz. *Pohřební homílie*. Olomouc: Matice Cyrilometodějská, 1998.

Smolík, J. *Kapitoly z liturgiky*. Praha: KEBF v Praze, 1960.

Šoltésová, V. "Misiológia v prostredí náboženského pluralizmu a sporné definície inkluzivistickej pozície." In *Principiálne východiská evanjelikálnej teológie. Zborník z Medzinárodnej vedeckej teologickej konferencie. – konanej 1. marca 2006*, 97–114. Banská Bystrica: KETM, 2006.

Stott, J. R. W. *Between Two Worlds: The Challenge of Preaching Today*. Grand Rapids; Cambridge, UK: Eerdmans, 1994.

———. *The Preacher´s Portrait*. Grand Rapids: Eerdmans, 1988.

Tureková, A. *Posledná rozlúčka*. Banská Bystrica: Združenie ZPOZ Človek-človeku v SR, ÚR, 2004.

———. *Každý deň stretnúť človeka. Metodicko-inštruktážny zborník, vydaný pri príležitosti 50. výročia vzniku zborov pre občianske záležitosti*. Banská Bystrica: Združenie ZPOZ Človek-človeku v SR, ÚR, 2003.

Wallis, Charles. *The Funeral Encyclopedia: A Source Book*. New York, Evanston, and London: Harper & Row, 1953.

Watson, J. *Pathway through Grief*. Crowborough, UK: Christina Press, 1997.

Winter, F. *Seelsorge an Sterbenden und Trauernden*. Berlin: Evangelische Verlagsanstalt, 1976.

Wislǿff, F. *Keď blízky odchádza*. Liptovský Mikuláš: Tranoscius, 2009.

Wood, R. Charles. *Sermon Outlines for Funeral Services*. Grand Rapids: Kregel, 1970.

Žák, V. A. *Malá praktická homiletika*. Praha: Evangelická církev metodistická, 1991.

Index

A

Aleš, P. 7, 21, 93, 104, 107, 134, 143,
150, 151

Axman, P. O. 7, 21, 93, 104, 107, 134,
143, 150, 151

B

Bohren, R. 4, 108, 120, 121, 123, 146

Briscoe, S. 125

C

Carr, W. 6, 25, 46, 47, 48, 49, 50, 51, 55,
57, 59, 66, 68, 69, 104, 141

Chapell, B. 76, 77, 93, 134, 135, 147,
148, 151

Connon, G. 38

D

Donnelly, P. 38

F

Fee, G. D. 119

Filo, J. 7, 12, 15, 21, 22, 27, 28, 53, 54,
61, 67, 77, 81, 88, 92, 101

G

Gennep, A. 64, 75

H

Hürlimann, C. 83, 90, 128

Hybels, B. 54, 125

J

Jamnický, J. 11, 18, 19, 21, 30, 31, 48,
62, 76, 77, 78, 79, 84, 107, 108,
109, 140, 142, 148, 150

Jenssen 13

Jenssen, H. H. 7, 13, 18, 71, 72, 73, 81,
82, 88, 91, 102, 103, 104, 128,
140, 143, 144, 149

K

Kavanagh, A. 62, 63

Kišš, I. 3, 5, 6, 25, 26, 31, 32, 35, 36, 46,
79, 89, 109, 112, 116, 132, 133

Kubíková, J. 92, 101, 107, 119, 134, 139

Kunz, R. 11

L

Long, T. G. 55, 56, 62, 145

Louw, J. P. 98

M

Malphurs, A. 2, 21, 29, 93, 136

Masarik, A. 9, 25, 26, 29, 110, 113, 133,
137

Melloh, J. A. 12, 27, 62, 63, 109, 119

Moltmann, J. 39, 55, 83, 84

P

Perry, L. M. 97, 142, 150

R

Robinson, H. W. 4, 7, 42, 54, 93, 125,
148

Rummage, S. 7, 21, 69, 70, 94

S

Senior, D. 91

Sheppy, P. xii, 6, 13, 38, 47, 49, 50, 53,
55, 61, 63, 65, 67, 69, 71, 75, 84,
141, 146

Smolík, J. 16, 49, 56, 81, 92, 99, 108,
109, 120, 121, 140, 141, 148

Šoltésová, V. 94

Stanček, Ľ. 4, 22

Stebler, C. 2, 6, 11, 14, 18, 21, 61, 70,
71, 108, 119, 129, 130, 133, 138,
143, 146, 149, 150

Sugden, H. F. 72, 73, 74, 75, 94, 102,
103, 105, 109, 134

V

Vrablec, J. 4, 91, 122, 124, 132

W

Wiersbe, W. 72, 73, 74, 75, 94, 102,
    103, 109, 134

Willhite, K. 29, 93, 136

Worden, J. W. 38

Wray, J. 27, 28, 52, 58, 70, 134

Z

Zemko, P. ix, 4, 93

Langham
PARTNERSHIP

Langham Literature and its imprints are a ministry of Langham Partnership.

Langham Partnership is a global fellowship working in pursuit of the vision God entrusted to its founder John Stott –

> *to facilitate the growth of the church in maturity and Christ-likeness through raising the standards of biblical preaching and teaching.*

Our vision is to see churches in the majority world equipped for mission and growing to maturity in Christ through the ministry of pastors and leaders who believe, teach and live by the Word of God.

Our mission is to strengthen the ministry of the Word of God through:
- nurturing national movements for biblical preaching
- fostering the creation and distribution of evangelical literature
- enhancing evangelical theological education

especially in countries where churches are under-resourced.

Our ministry

Langham Preaching partners with national leaders to nurture indigenous biblical preaching movements for pastors and lay preachers all around the world. With the support of a team of trainers from many countries, a multi-level programme of seminars provides practical training, and is followed by a programme for training local facilitators. Local preachers' groups and national and regional networks ensure continuity and ongoing development, seeking to build vigorous movements committed to Bible exposition.

Langham Literature provides majority world preachers, scholars and seminary libraries with evangelical books and electronic resources through publishing and distribution, grants and discounts. The programme also fosters the creation of indigenous evangelical books in many languages, through writer's grants, strengthening local evangelical publishing houses, and investment in major regional literature projects, such as one volume Bible commentaries like *The Africa Bible Commentary* and *The South Asia Bible Commentary*.

Langham Scholars provides financial support for evangelical doctoral students from the majority world so that, when they return home, they may train pastors and other Christian leaders with sound, biblical and theological teaching. This programme equips those who equip others. Langham Scholars also works in partnership with majority world seminaries in strengthening evangelical theological education. A growing number of Langham Scholars study in high quality doctoral programmes in the majority world itself. As well as teaching the next generation of pastors, graduated Langham Scholars exercise significant influence through their writing and leadership.

To learn more about Langham Partnership and the work we do visit **langham.org**

www.ingramcontent.com/pod-product-compliance
Lightning Source LLC
Chambersburg PA
CBHW070918270326
41927CB00011B/2626